family table

Also by Shaye Elliott:

Welcome to the Farm

From Scratch

FARM
COOKING
from the ELLIOTT
HOMESTEAD

family table

SHAYE ELLIOTT

Foreword by Stuart Elliott

Guilford, Connecticut

An imprint of Globe Pequot

Distributed by NATIONAL BOOK NETWORK

Photograph on page vii by Mary Collier
All other photographs by Shaye Elliott

British Library Cataloguing in Publication Information available

Library of Congress Cataloging-in-Publication Data

Names: Elliott, Shaye, author. | Elliott Homestead.
Title: Family table : farm cooking from the Elliott Homestead / Shaye Elliott
 ; foreword by Stuart Elliott.
Description: Guilford, Connecticut : Lyons Press, [2018] | Includes index.
Identifiers: LCCN 2017043233 (print) | LCCN 2017050623 (ebook) |
ISBN 9781493031535 (e-book) | ISBN 9781493031528 (paperback) |
ISBN   9781493031535 (ebook)
Subjects: LCSH: Cooking, American. | LCGFT: Cookbooks.
Classification: LCC TX715 (ebook) | LCC TX715 .E465 2018 (print) | DDC
 641.5973—dc23
LC record available at https://lccn.loc.gov/2017043233

∞™ The paper used in this publication meets the minimum requirements of American National Standard for Information Sciences—Permanence of Paper for Printed Library Materials, ANSI/NISO Z39.48-1992.

Printed in the United States of America

THIS BOOK IS DEDICATED TO MY CHILDREN.

May this life that we're sharing with you take root in your hearts and flourish!

CONTENTS

Soups and Salads

Side Dishes

Main Dishes

Sweets

A Mix of Goodies

FOREWORD

by Stuart Elliott

When I first started playing the guitar, my fingers ached as they built up strength, developing blisters and calluses. I remember the muted sound of the strings as I tried to strum a chord with only enough finger strength to make it sound like some strange percussion instrument. But I also remember the feeling I had the first time I, almost unexpectedly, played through a song without a mistake.

When the sound from the guitar faded away and silence consumed my empty bedroom, there was no one there to cheer or congratulate me; but there didn't need to be. The song itself, played through with harmonious sound, was celebration enough. If I am still for a moment and take some time to reflect, I can think of many more things in my life that served as culminating celebrations. They develop like images in my mind's eye. I see a soccer ball, a diploma, a paycheck, a wedding aisle, a newborn girl, a garden, a meal. I remember, and I smile inside and out because I see how they have been building to a singular point.

Not everything in our lives culminates in a celebration like this. There are parts of life that we might not ever get the gratification of seeing how they will all come together. A lot of what we do is with a mind toward a future we know we will never see, but we retain hope for others that they may see it and celebrate in it. Sometimes it isn't clear what we are working toward or what our goals are. Sometimes things are done out of necessity without thinking of the sense of satisfaction that may or may not come from them. But then there are those things that bring their own reward; those things that are a celebration in themselves. These culminating celebrations, like the song, can be small and even unexpected. Or, they can be quite big and culminate in an important event. I have come to see that every meal we have, whether it is small and quickly thrown together or a big planned family dinner, is a culminating celebration. Preparing meals for your family should not be one of those things that is purposeless, without direction or joy. I sincerely think that if anyone can help you celebrate at your table, with your family, Shaye can, as many of you already know. She can because she has not only put thought into the ingredients for her recipes, she has also cultivated them and cared for them, growing with them. In every meal you serve from this book, she is celebrating along with you.

What Shaye has put together for you between these two covers is more than a book of recipes: It is a culminating celebration, one that we humbly hope you will join in.

Every celebration has a story behind it, a story of struggle and conflict, of perseverance and resolve. Should a cookbook be any different? (Is the story behind our meals any different?) Each dish, prepared and documented here for you to enjoy, has its own story, a significant part of which takes place on our homestead. Behind that Chicken Piccata you'll cook for your family on Friday was a day of digging fence postholes. The pears used in the Red Wine and Honey-Poached Pears photograph were chosen from a basketful of pears that already had greedy little teeth marks in most of them. Sorrow accompanies the lamb recipe. Hope is entwined with every Tommy Toe tomato. Every meal you make that incorporates even the smallest part of this story is a mini-celebration of its own.

Many of you reading this are already familiar with our story, and now you are excited that you have a new and special way to be a part of it. As you walk through these pages you will add chapters to the stories behind your own meals. Some of you may have a similar story to ours; the setting and the characters will be familiar. You will jump into this flood of food and photos and the water will be just right for you. Some of you are looking for a new story or for a way to connect to your favorite kind of story. As you turn the pages of this book, you will find what you are looking for. Whatever the case may be, I can say with confidence that my darling wife, Shaye, has created something for you. It comes to you with history, love and loss, tears and joy, triumph and struggle. And those are the best kinds of stories, because they touch on something real. And that is something we all want and need.

A foreword, apparently, is supposed to be written by someone credible. Other than being a part of the author's everyday life, having tasted every dish, inhaled their gorgeous smells, beheld their aesthetic beauty, and relied on them to sustain and nourish me throughout my days, my credentials are lacking. But I am connected to every word and every picture like no one else is. And, for what it's worth, I think what you are holding is something very special. Something to be celebrated. But that's the unbiased opinion of a proud husband. Please enjoy! I know you will.

Welcome to the Farm

There was a moment when our family sat down at the dinner table and I stood back for a second, released a deep sigh that can come only after a day of hard labor, and looked at the overflowing spread set before us.

The soup we were eating had a base made from chicken stock simmered with root vegetables from our winter storage, and the carcass from one of our homegrown meat birds. The carrots, onions, and potatoes I had whipped into a gratin were from our larder, grown just ten yards from the kitchen door. The meat was sausage made that day from our very own pigs, butchered just a month prior in our barnyard. Sally Belle, our family cow back then, had provided the butter and buttermilk for the fresh-baked buttermilk biscuits.

Ninety percent of the protein had been raised . . . grown . . . harvested . . . preserved right here on The Elliott Homestead. Wow. We'd *done it*. We had done what we set out to achieve years ago: We had become producers.

It's moments like this when I feel deeply grateful for our teeny little farm and all of its potential. Even though we're nestled on just five acres, most of which is still undeveloped, we've been able to transform where our food comes from, how it's grown, the footprint it leaves behind, and, most important, how it tastes!

I must admit, after eating almost all our own food, I've become something of a fresh food connoisseur. *Fresh* to me means harvested from the garden or collected from the chicken coop *that very day*. *Fresh* means eating everything in season, as and when it grows in nature. *Fresh* means filling a pail with milk and making hot chocolate with it that same evening. *Fresh* means it was born, raised, and butchered right here on the farm, every day of its life filled with fresh air and sunshine and plenty of room to roam. As a foodie, that's what it's all about it in my book—the simplest, most delicious, purest form of food available.

I suppose it's safe for me to assume that since you've read at least this far, you, too, must have a passion for this kind of food. You know the kind I'm talking about: It's the type of food that sings—and makes you want to sing! Some of us choose to produce it ourselves, and some choose to obtain it through local organic farms, community supported agriculture, and farmers' markets. It's amazing what we can source from our own communities and the impact that kind of "shopping" can have on our local economies—and on our bellies. Because on top of the many benefits it brings to the farmers we buy from, let's face the facts: Fresh food just tastes better.

The Gardens

My first garden was a humble 6 x 3-foot bed that my husband Stuart built for me at our first rental house shortly after we were married. It sat in a sunny corner of an otherwise completely run-down yard and was a beacon of hope in that disheveled neighborhood in Washington State. It sprouted some of the most luscious tomatoes I've grown to date, and I'd like to think those tomatoes encouraged me along this path. After all, I was a complete novice. Planting peas in July and peppers in March—what did I know? And yet, I harvested a fair bit of produce from that little bed, even enough to tackle my first ever canning project—homemade salsa. I remember looking out our kitchen window one day and seeing the sun's rays shining through the tendrils of a climbing pea and thinking, *This is it. This is what I love. This is what I want.* My poor husband didn't know what he was in for.

When we moved a few short months after my garden began to die back in the fall, I convinced Stu to help me transfer the soil and garden box to our new rental house. He, being a newlywed, lovingly obliged by shoveling pickup truckloads of soil and driving it five miles away. Our new home offered us more yard space for gardening, and eventually we built six more identical garden beds. We planted one with strawberries, another with peppers, another with squash, peas, and lettuce, and yet another with tomatoes and garlic.

I spent two growing seasons at this home, continuing to learn and sharpen my still-very-green gardening skills. I slowly began to learn the flow of the harvest and understand the rhythm of the seasons: Arugula was planted in the early spring, soon to be followed by the lettuces and spinach. Heat-loving plants, such as eggplant, peppers, and tomatoes, shouldn't venture outside until well into May. The peas needed to be harvested regularly, lest they become slightly bitter and stringy. The garlic needed an extra thick layer of mulch to keep them evenly moist throughout the summer. I kept herbs by the kitchen window for easy access and began to learn the joys of saving seeds from heirloom vegetables.

I wasn't a *great* gardener, but I loved it and kept at it, learning to preserve whatever we grew on our teeny-tiny plot.

After a few years at that house, we moved once again, this time, to lower Alabama. A new climate, a new zone, a new gardening experience altogether. Because of the intense tree canopy along Mobile Bay, and the fact that our entire "lawn" was made of sand, not much gardening happened there. I tried to force a few kale plants into pots. They weren't havin' it. Instead of growing my own produce that year, I found a few local farmers who were willing to sell me plump bags of their organic produce from the back of their pickup trucks. Each week I made the short drive to their farms, loaded up the trunk of my minivan, and went home with a bounty of kale, pecans, collards, citrus fruit, broccoli, turnips, persimmons, peanuts, and sweet potatoes. It was then that I began to understand the importance of community in agriculture. I didn't have the means to do any of this production myself, and yet, there were still people who were able and willing to sell to me!

I couldn't have a garden of my own, but I could walk the fields with a farmer named Chip every week and put money for his produce right into his pocket.

I couldn't keep bees, but I could pick up a gallon of local raw honey from a nearby beekeeper who sold the most delicious wildflower honey I've ever tasted.

I couldn't raise meat chickens, but I could source them from a local producer who prided himself on the quality of life his birds had.

I couldn't keep laying hens, but I could pick up my weekly five dozen at Penny's house, where chickens ran all around the yard, leaving cash in the fridge of her in-home hair salon.

There's no need to wait until you've got the perfect space for gardening. There are many plants that are well suited for small growing spaces—such as peppers, onions, and lettuce. Grow what you can, where you are, with what you have.

The community—the conscious decision to do business directly with those producers—added a richness to our food that I'd never experienced before. It wasn't just a fried egg for breakfast. It was an egg from one of those silly Silkies that roamed Penny's yard. It wasn't just a bunch of collard greens, it was the last of the collards that we'd see for the season, harvested the day before, while my kids scampered through the rows in the waning light.

Our food began to have a story.

We decided we wanted to pursue this food with a story. We landed on our first farm (not our last) shortly after—a small double-wide on five acres of hilly, uncultivated land. Our first order of business was to get some produce growing, so straight away our first garden bed went in, even before we'd unpacked the boxes of underwear and towels.

It started small, a 10 x 4-foot bed edged with random rocks we'd found around the scrubby yard.

Keep great garden notes! If you document your most delicious produce, you'll know which varieties to grow the following year for an even tastier garden. I like to track planting dates, varieties grown, and total amount harvested.

The following spring we expanded that to a 500-square-foot bed, surrounded by recycled posts and poultry wire to keep the new laying hens away from the valuable plants. Later on that summer we added yet another 400-square-foot bed. And by the fall, a 200-square-foot greenhouse was included in the mix.

Fast-forward a few years and we've now landed on 2.25 beautiful (irrigated) acres just down the road from our first farm. This land has been cultivated to meet our vegetable, meat, egg, and dairy needs.

On these tiny plots of land, we've been able to grow more produce than we can eat ourselves, so we opted to share or barter much of the extra.

Tommy Toe, Yellow Pear, Brandywine, Italian Heirloom, and Gold Metal tomatoes line up in neat rows before they grow too heavy, bowing and flopping over the entire garden.

Provider green beans climb the garden fence, winding and twisting in the most artful dance toward the sun.

Amish Pie squash explode over the southwest corner of the bed, where they remain until fall (and pie time!) arrives.

Detroit Red and Bull's Blood beets provide us with fresh greens all summer long, before we pull them from their snug beds. Some are pickled, others are eaten fresh or fermented, and a few will remain in a bed of loose soil for winter meals.

Peas, watermelon, potatoes, horseradish, rhubarb, broccoli, cabbage, zinnia blossoms, cucumbers, basil, rosemary, parsley, thyme, currants, strawberries, raspberries, gooseberries, onions, shallots, tomatillos, chile pepper, bell peppers, eggplants, pumpkins, zucchini. The list goes on.

From a small, corner garden bed to over 2000 square feet of garden in just a few short years. That's a lot of work. That's a lot of compost. That's a lot of produce.

And that's a lot of delicious eating.

What's Growing in the Garden?

Our gardens serve one purpose: to feed our family. Naturally if we were growing for a market, they would look and function much differently. But since it's just us and our palates, we get to explore and work them as we wish. Our casual gardening style is reflected in my less-than-perfected planting schedule and lax weeding habits. But since they continue to produce the food that we need year after year, I see no reason to hold them to a more rigorous plan. And while the varieties and methods of gardens and gardeners are as numerous as stars in the sky, here's a general idea of what our garden grows:

Cabbage	Greens	Hops	Pears
Beans	Tomatoes	Eggplant	Shallots
Potatoes	Peas	Peppers	Broccoli
Onions	Garlic	Berries	Cauliflower
Herbs	Carrots	Currants	Artichokes
Brussels sprouts	Flowers	Gooseberries	
Cucumbers	Squash	Plums	

Tips for Buying Great Produce

Know your grower: Quite simply, one of the easiest ways to get the best produce is simply to know who you're buying it from. Whether this means roadside stands, or a coworker with extra in her garden, knowing exactly where your produce is grown will get you the best results. Establishing a relationship with that grower, or several growers, is even better, as they'll often call to fill you in on crop performance and preparation tips.

Shop in season: It sounds so elementary to say this, but the reality is that in our culture, we've worked hard to de-establish seasonal eating. Strawberries are available in December. You can buy tomatoes all year round. Because produce is routinely being shipped from hundreds, even thousands of miles away, the flavor and freshness inevitably suffers. In fact, many varieties have been developed expressly for travel and storage rather than flavor. Yes, really.

Adopting a seasonal eating cycle with your produce will not only ensure you get the best the season has to offer, but it also allows you the freedom and joy of learning about new vegetables and experimenting with new flavors. Instead of just choosing lettuce from the grocery store all year, how about chard in the summer, collards in the fall, kale in the winter, and lettuce in the spring? There's a whole, wide world of vegetables out there just waiting to be explored and devoured!

Hit up a farmers' market: The easiest way to get the best produce is simply to stop by your local market. These markets are specifically designed to help bring farm-fresh goodness to your plate. And if you're shopping the market, you're naturally shopping in season and will likely meet your grower. See how beautifully this community works? Stop looking to your grocery store and instead, put that money right into the farmers' pockets. They've got better produce anyway!

Get over the bugs: Believe it or not, some cultures prefer their vegetables nibbled on by bugs. Why? Because insects often choose the best-tasting vegetables, of course! Our greens are frequently speckled with cabbage worms or earwigs. Ain't no thing. Flick 'em off and get over the holes that are dotting your cabbage leaves. Good produce is still good produce—no need to waste it. On top of that, bug presence may even indicate organic produce, unlike commercially grown, bug-free fruits and vegetables, which have been doused with enough insecticide to drop a small horse. So if it's got bugs, most of the time it means it's good eating for you, too!

Shop for flavor: And speaking of good eating, when was the last time you *tasted* your vegetables *before* you bought them? My guess is that you rarely, if ever, perform the taste test. Why not? If you're buying food to eat it, you better make sure it tastes good. Farmers are often eager and willing to share a bite. One of my favorite farmers, Farmer Steve, welcomed me onto his farm with a fresh ear of his super-sweet corn. Plucked right from the stalk. And you know what? Because it tasted good, I bought thirty ears of it. Food is about flavor, not size or uniformity, so don't forget that when you're shopping.

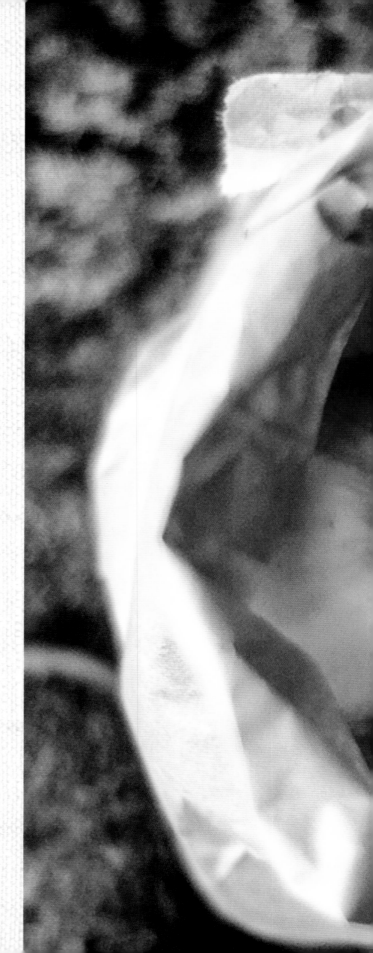

The Dairy

It wasn't until we moved to our farm that we began to explore the radical and political world that is the home dairy. Raw milk is a bit of a black market product these days, and its purchase often results in back-alley exchanges. We've been avid raw milk enthusiasts for years, even choosing to buy those gallons labeled "For Pet Consumption Only" while living in a state where the sale of raw milk had been deemed unlawful.

How on Earth our culture can support eating squirtable, shelf-stable cheese product yet simultaneously fear raw milk is beyond me. But that's a whole other story.

Our novice dairy ventures resulted in much trial and heartache, as most of these early forays usually do. Our first dairy cow, Kula, had supposedly

been bred before she arrived on the farm, but ol' rookie me didn't think to have a vet confirm her condition, and it turned out, she wasn't. I had fallen for an old marketing ploy. After four failed attempts at artificial insemination and several escapades with a bull, Kula was still "open" (not with calf). Kula was obviously not getting us any closer to our goal of homegrown raw milk, and thus, she . . . well, let's just say she had to find a different place to live on the farm.

Our second cow, and one of the loves of my life, was Sally Belle. Sally came to us from a family a few hours away who had raised her as a 4-H show cow and had utilized her incredible mothering ability to raise fat and sassy calves each year. And I can see why—Sally's milk was more than 30 percent cream. *Cream,* people.

The ebb and flow of the home dairy was a steep learning curve for me. How does one milk a cow when, after all, one has never done it before?

I've always been a jump-in-the-deep-end kinda gal. Learning to love, care for, and milk Sal was no exception. She arrived on our farm in milk, and we had two hours to acquaint ourselves with her before tucking up under her flank for our first milking session. Which, by the way, went horribly wrong. But that's another story for another time.

Sally became the queen of our little kingdom here, ruling the roost, if you will. Sally's milk provided our family with cheese, kefir, buttermilk, yogurt, butter, cream, and milk. Her extra milk fattened hogs and many batches of meat chickens, raised a bottle-fed lamb, and gave the dogs something to look forward to each time I cleaned out the milk fridge. Her manure fertilized the gardens and the pastures. We maintained her on alfalfa and grass hay. Sal only wanted a small bit of rolled oats at each milking.

Sally was my lifetime farm dream in bovine form, but more than that, she was my friend. When one spends hours upon hours upon hours tucked under the flank of a dairy cow, one becomes very attached to her smell . . . her temperament . . . her, fine I'll say it, udder. I knew Sally's teats like the back of my hand. Man, this is a strange life.

After enjoying her milk and companionship for a few years on our farm, we had to say good-bye to our sweet Sal after an unexpected injury. I wept for weeks. To bond and commune with a dairy animal is to connect with another soul. I still miss her terribly.

We've since welcomed a new dairy queen to the farm, another beautiful Jersey named Cecelia. This year she blessed us with her first calf, a little heifer named Pepper. Though our relationship with Cece is in its infancy, we look forward to many years tucked under her flanks in milking glory.

I'll openly admit that the dairy is my favorite part of the farm. Maybe it's because the dairy cows understand what I've been going through as a mother of four these past years. We relate to each other.

And then, of course, we eat butter.

The Meat

Among the most rewarding, if not *the* most rewarding, aspects of our farming has been meat production. Dare I say, it's also been the easiest. And with the high prices and unsustainable options available at the supermarket, it's also been the product I couldn't wait to quit buying completely. I just won't support large commercial feeding operations with my dollars.

Did you know that I used to work at a feedlot? It's true. Can you even believe that? After graduating from college with a degree in animal science, I began working on a local feedlot as part of a bold future that revolved around commercial agriculture and beef production. It didn't take long for me to start asking questions. Why were these animals sick all the time? Why did their diet consist of almost no grass? Why were we shipping in semi-loads of corn and food waste, when there were thousands of acres of pasture right here? Why was this land barren and dead? What was the responsible thing to do with all that animal waste?

My questions, and the simple answers to them, went unsatisfied. And thus began my sustainable, grass-based meat production ideals.

Here on the farm, just a few short years in, we've been able to produce *all* of our family's animal protein needs. Pork, chicken, rabbit, and lamb reign supreme, with the option for beef (depending on whether our cow throws us a bull or heifer calf). In our little world, grass is king. Supplemented with locally sourced organic grain and organic garden scraps, it's an incredibly efficient and sustainable production process.

Our small herd of Katahdin sheep gives us the most remarkably tender, flavorful lamb. We're continuing to grow our herd because our love for their meat continues to grow. Our sheep are raised on pasture and hay, spend their days in the sun, and are killed right here on our farm. Although lamb isn't as popular in the United States, worldwide, it's extremely popular. Our local "lamb skeptics" are quickly converted when they try it. Their tasty meat is due in part to the amount of lanolin in their hides. Katahdin are a "hair" sheep, meaning they don't grow fleece like a traditional sheep, which results in a bit less sheep-y flavor.

The fact that we're not enjoying more of this succulent protein should be a crime. Any visitor to my farm will be stuffed full of a properly prepared roast before being sent out into the world to preach about the mighty power that is lamb.

Along with our sheep are the hogs we raise each year. You just can't beat the value of raising a pig. They're basically garbage disposals . . . that give you bacon. Our pigs are grazed and fattened on extra milk, garden waste, spoiled vegetables, kitchen scraps, old bread, gleaned fruit from the nearby orchards, and a bit of locally sourced organic grain.

The amount of meat and value that comes from the pig is remarkable. Because almost every single bit of it is edible, almost none is wasted. Odd bits are used to feed the farm dogs, and I've been learning to cook the less common cuts that one only gets to experience when butchering the animal firsthand.

How's the taste of homegrown pork? Forget about it. I mean it. Forget what you know of commercial pork and enter into an entirely new world of porcine pleasure.

The meat chickens we raise a few times a year, I'll admit, are not my favorites. Birds are just sort of weird. And stinky, even on the best of days in the tidiest environments. However, their meat is worth enduring their feathery little presence. We raise about sixty broilers each year, which provide us with a little more than a chicken per week. This is the perfect amount for our family right now, although as these children grow bigger, so will our need for chicken!

We use the chicken livers for pâté. The feet, necks, and carcasses make a few gallons of homemade chicken stock each week. Feathers and blood are composted for garden fertilizer. Kidneys, gizzards, and other odd bits are fed to the dogs. Nothing is wasted, because it all gives back to the farm in its own unique way.

I've yet to find something that makes me happier than sitting down with a homegrown, roasted chicken and a bottle of local IPA beer. It's my happy place. Greasy fingers and all.

The rabbits are another incredibly sustainable and efficient meat for us to grow on the farm. Not only do rabbits reproduce easily and quickly (they are, after all, rabbits), but they fatten just as quickly and easily on the cheapest of feeds: hay, weeds, grass, and yard clippings. We're trading weeds for meat, people! Isn't that incredible?

Our current rabbitry includes three does and one buck, which provide us with new rabbits quite often! After only a few months of munchin' grass, they're ready for harvest. Rabbit meat is a lean, mild-tasting protein that lends itself well to soups, stews, and casseroles. Layered with homemade bacon and herbs and roasted alongside garden vegetables, the taste will keep up with the best of 'em.

Meat production isn't too complicated. Even those of you living within city limits may be surprised at the amount you're able to grow on your little patch of earth. If growing meat isn't your thing, that's okay too. Local producers and direct-sale farms are popping up all over the country. Find a farmer near you who grows quality meats, and use your dollars to support his or her products and operation. It matters.

Questions to Ask Your Meat Producer

Are your animals raised on pasture? This question opens up a larger conversation about pasture management, rotational grazing, fertilization, and animal health. When an animal has access to pasture, it most likely also has access to grazing, sunshine, fresh air, and a variety of vegetation. A well-managed, grazing, free-roaming animal is a generally healthy animal.

Are your animals organic? I'm not of the mindset that an animal has to be organic to be good. That being said, this question will help you better understand the farmer's methods and priorities. For example, we sometimes feed our broiler chickens a nonorganic feed. Even though the feed is not certified organic, it's not sprayed, is sourced from local farmers, and is GMO-free. This is a great option for us to keep our chicken raising cost-effective while still utilizing some of the best feed we can access. It's a great conversation to have with your farmer. If nothing else, you'll hear his or her opinion on the organic certification process.

Were your animals born on your farm? If they weren't, where did they come from? Another farm down the road? Across the country? Out of the country? At the risk of sounding like a control freak, I don't have a lot of trust in marketing, so I prefer to buy from farms that I can see, touch, and feel. It's the only way to ensure I'm getting what I pay for. There's nothing fundamentally wrong with bringing animals onto a farm from elsewhere, but this question will alert the farmer that you care and want to purchase from a place you can get behind.

Have your animals ever been given antibiotics? Antibiotics have a place in modern society, but in our animals' feed is not one of them. Sometimes, particularly after an injury, antibiotics can be a true lifesaver. In today's agricultural system, however, they're used as a bandage to cover poor management techniques and decisions. Talk to your farmer about how he or she cares for sick animals and what his or her thoughts are on antibiotics.

How are your animals finished? *Finished* is simply a fancy word for *fattened*. Has the animal been finished on grain? On grass? On pellets? On whole grains? Most likely, if it's been commercially grown, the animal will have been finished on an incredibly low grass-to-grain ratio, with corn and soy making up the majority of its diet. This is unsustainable and unnecessary for foraging, grass-loving animals like cows. Question your farmer's finishing practices and find one whose methods you can support.

Did the animal have friends? Just kidding. Ha! But it couldn't hurt.

Up with the Sun

It's never fun pulling my body from the warm cocoon of the bed when it longs to slumber just a bit longer. And yet, there's something about the early moments of the morning that I just can't resist. Perhaps it's the slivers of light that crest the mountain ridge nearby and last only for a fleeting, picturesque moment. Perhaps, at least for part of the year, it's the low, steady mooing of our dairy cow as she awaits her morning milking and breakfast. Or perhaps it's the first crow of that gangly ol' rooster that refuses to leave our homestead. But most likely, let's just admit it now, it's the coffee.

The fresh roast is hand ground each morning before it's scooped into our favorite French press to drown in boiling water. Five minutes later, the plunger in the French press goes down and that heavenly liquid rises up. It's poured into my favorite brown and cream colored English teacup. It's sipped. It's savored. It's soul-reviving.

My teacup and I usually sit in the big cushy chair where we watch the sun rise, pray the toddlers sleep in, and catch up on the day's inevitable tasks with my husband. Every day of the week, we find a few minutes each morning for this routine—a routine that encourages, recharges, and guides our day.

breakfast
and
breads

CRUSTY HASH BROWNS

Serves 4 to 6

2 pounds russet
potatoes, peeled

3 tablespoons tallow,
butter, or lard

1 teaspoon sea salt

Freshly ground
black pepper

1 tablespoon olive oil

Fresh herbs, for garnish

Mmm . . . crusty potatoes. One of my many culinary kryptonites. Serve them as is or top them with sliced cherry tomatoes, pesto, grilled vegetables, or eggs. Imagine the possibilities!

Grate the potatoes using a box grater. Transfer the grated potatoes into a colander and squeeze out as much liquid as possible.

Heat the tallow, butter, or lard in a large, cast-iron skillet over medium heat.

In a large bowl, toss the grated potatoes with the salt, pepper, and olive oil. Carefully place the potatoes in the hot skillet, gently spreading them evenly around the skillet. Let the potatoes cook for 10 to 15 minutes without stirring them—the potatoes should be cooked through on top and fused into a hash brown on the bottom.

Place a large plate over the top of the skillet. Carefully flip the skillet over so the hash brown slides onto the plate. Slide the hash brown back into the skillet, uncooked side down. Cook for 10 to 15 minutes more, until crispy and golden.

Transfer hash brown to a large platter and cut into wedges. Garnish with freshly chopped herbs, if desired. And might I suggest a perfectly poached egg, right on top? Have mercy!

EGG AND GARDEN TOMATO SAMMIES

Serves 4

I enjoy these sandwiches all through the summer months, when tomatoes are at their peak! During the winter I'll often substitute sun-dried tomatoes. Devoured with crusty bread that's been slathered with herbed butter? Fuggedaboutit.

Preheat the oven to 450°F.

Melt 3 tablespoons of the butter in a small saucepan. When melted, remove from heat, add the freshly chopped herbs and gently stir. Spoon the herb butter onto the bread slices, using the back of the spoon to smear evenly.

Arrange the buttered bread slices on a baking sheet and place in the oven for 5 minutes, or until toasted and golden.

While the bread is toasting, heat a medium cast-iron skillet. Add the remaining 1 tablespoon butter. Gently crack the eggs into the skillet and cook for 2 minutes. Using a spatula, flip the eggs over and cook for another 2 minutes.

Remove the bread from the oven. Place an egg atop four of the bread slices. Arrange a few of those delicious tomato slices atop each egg. Close each sandwich with the remaining slices of herby, buttery toasted bread and enjoy!

4 tablespoons butter, divided

3 teaspoons freshly chopped herbs, such as rosemary, chives, thyme, and oregano

8 slices crusty bread

4 eggs

1 large tomato, thinly sliced

PLUM CLAFOUTIS

Serves 4

10–15 ripe plums, pitted
and cut in half

6 tablespoons
dehydrated whole
cane sugar, divided

3 eggs

1⅓ cups whole milk
(or cream if you're
up for it!)

⅓ cup organic, all-
purpose, unbleached
flour or sprouted
whole wheat flour

1 teaspoon freshly
grated lemon zest

1 tablespoon vanilla
extract

Small pinch of sea salt

Small pinch of freshly
grated nutmeg

Sounds fancy, but throwing this dish together is anything but complicated. Fresh fruit. A few basic ingredients. Magic.

Preheat the oven to 375°F.

Place the plums, cut side down, in a baking dish. Sprinkle with 3 tablespoons of the dehydrated whole cane sugar.

In a food processor or high-powered blender, blend together the remaining 3 tablespoons of dehydrated whole cane sugar, eggs, milk, flour, lemon zest, vanilla, salt, and nutmeg. Blend for 1 minute, or until frothy and well combined. Pour the egg mixture over the plums.

Transfer the dish to the oven and bake for 50 to 60 minutes, or until fragrant and golden. The clafoutis will puff up as it cooks, so you can turn on the interior oven light, pull up a chair, and watch the magic happen. Not that any sane person would do such a thing. Ahem.

GOLDEN PORRIDGE
WITH PEAR

Serves 6–8

There's something about this dish that feels like being wrapped in a warm woolen blanket. I'll take that as a win.

Combine the barley, quinoa, oats, sesame seeds, and flax seeds in a large bowl. Add the cider vinegar and water until all the solids are completely submerged. Gently stir, cover with a tea towel, and set aside to soak at room temperature for 12 hours. After the soaking period, carefully pour off any remaining water.

Preheat the oven to 350°F.

Add the syrup, salt, and chopped pear to the grain mixture and gently stir to combine.

In a separate bowl, whisk together the milk and eggs, add to the grains, and stir to combine.

Pour the porridge mixture into a buttered baking dish. Sprinkle with the almonds and pecans. Place in the oven and bake for 45 minutes, or until deeply golden.

Serve warm with a dollop of vanilla yogurt and a generous drizzle of raw honey.

1 cup barley

1 cup quinoa, rinsed

1 cup oats

½ cup sesame seeds

½ cup flax seeds

1 tablespoon raw apple cider vinegar

Filtered water

⅓ cup maple syrup

1 teaspoon sea salt

1 cup chopped pear or other seasonal fruit

1½ cups milk

5 eggs

Butter, for baking

¼ cup almonds

¼ cup pecans

Vanilla yogurt, for serving

Raw honey, for serving

BREAKFAST QUINOA WITH EGGS AND SMOKED HOLLANDAISE SAUCE

Serves 4

1 cup quinoa, rinsed

2 cups filtered water

4 slices bacon

1 tablespoon butter

4 eggs

Smoked Hollandaise Sauce (see page 196)

If you want to impress in a major way, make this for breakfast. Or for lunch. Or for dinner. When it's been drizzled in a smoky hollandaise, there are no rules.

Combine the quinoa and water in a small saucepan. Bring to a low simmer, cover, and simmer for 10 minutes, or until the quinoa is tender.

Meanwhile, in a cast-iron skillet, fry the bacon until crispy, 3 to 5 minutes per side.

In a separate cast-iron skillet, melt the butter and fry the eggs gently until they're cooked but the yolks remain runny.

Spoon ½ cup of the cooked quinoa onto each of four plates. Top each pile of quinoa with one egg. Drizzle with a few tablespoons of Smoked Hollandaise Sauce. Crumble one piece of bacon over the top of the sauce and add a twist of freshly ground pepper.

Die of breakfast (or lunch or dinner) happiness.

LEMON-BERRY CREAM SCONES

Makes 8

I'm a sucker for these scones. The earthiness of the spelt. The zing of the berries. The warmth of the vanilla. Stick a fork in me—I'm done!

Preheat the oven to 400°F.

Whisk together the flours, baking powder, and sea salt in a bowl.

In a separate bowl, mix together the cream, maple syrup, and vanilla.

Add the berries and lemon zest to the dry flour mixture. Gently stir. Pour the cream mixture into the flour mixture and use a fork to gently combine. If it's too runny, add a bit more of the all-purpose flour to get it to the right consistency. It should be a loose, shaggy ball.

Turn the dough out onto a floured countertop and gently knead into a ball. Use your palms to gently smoosh the ball into a disk shape.

Using a large knife, cut the disk into eight equal wedges, like a pizza. Place the wedges on a parchment-lined baking sheet. Brush with the melted butter and drizzle lightly with the honey. Bake for 16 to 18 minutes, until just golden, before removing to a wire rack to cool. Try not to burn your fingers as you tear into the scones like a ravenous wolf.

1 cup organic, unbleached all-purpose flour, plus extra, as needed

1 cup sprouted spelt flour

2½ teaspoons baking powder

½ teaspoon sea salt

1⅓ cups cream

⅓ cup maple syrup

1 teaspoon vanilla

½ cup berries, fresh or frozen

1 lemon, zested

3 tablespoons butter, melted

3 tablespoons honey

HOMEMADE HAM

Makes approximately 12 servings

1 fresh pork roast, preferably from the leg (you can get this cut from your local butcher)

Sea salt

Dehydrated whole cane sugar

Honey, molasses, or herbs

Curing meat the traditional way (that is, with salt) has become a new favorite pastime of ours on the farm. Pork lends itself well to this curing technique and never ceases to amaze me. This homemade ham recipe can be used on any pork roast, though the traditional ham cut comes from the butt and leg of the pig.

Dry the roast with a rag to absorb any extra moisture. Weigh the roast and write down this number. For every pound of meat, weigh out 1 tablespoon sea salt and ½ teaspoon sugar. Combine them in a bowl; use your fingers to mix them together.

Rub the pork with the salt–sugar mixture. Be sure to get it into every nook and cranny. Really work it in there. If you have a bone-in roast, pay special attention to that area. You want the meat to be evenly covered.

Measure the diameter of the roast at its thickest part and add 3 to figure out how many days it will cure. For example, a roast that is 7 inches across will cure for 7+3 = 10 days total.

Transfer the pork roast to a large bowl, place in the refrigerator, and let the roast be—the salt will do its magic. After the proper curing time, remove the ham. At this point, the ham can be baked in a 350°F oven until the internal temperature is roughly 170°F to 180°F. It can be glazed with honey or molasses or sprinkled with herbs. Alternatively, the ham can be smoked to the same internal temperature.

HOMEMADE BACON—
DRY-CURED AND AIR-DRIED

You haven't tasted bacon until you've experienced dry-cured bacon. The salt pulls the water from the meat, condensing the flavors of the fatty pork. It only takes a teeny bit of care and yields incredible results. This recipe may be the entire reason we raise pigs.

Dehydrated whole cane sugar, about 6 cups

Coarse sea salt, about 6 cups

Fresh pork belly from the best quality hog you can find (if you can't grow your own pig, try to find a local pork farmer)

Large, plastic bin

In a large bowl with a tight-fitting lid, combine the sugar and salt. Generously rub the flesh side of the pork belly with the mixture. Rub the sugar–salt mix into the flesh some more. Did I mention you need to rub the ol' pork belly down with the sugar and salt? The sides too. Make sure to get any pockets or under bits of fat—anywhere water could accumulate. Cover the remaining sugar–salt mix and set aside until needed.

Stack the pork belly slab (or slabs) into the plastic bin. Stick it in the refrigerator and forget about it until the next day. Dump the accumulated liquid out of the bin and rub the flesh with the sugar–salt mix. Put the pork back into the tub and stick it in the fridge again. The next day, dump out any accumulated liquid and rub the sugar–salt mix on any part of the pork belly where the salt and sugar has completely dissolved. A thin layer will do. Repeat this process every day until liquid stops accumulating in the bin. This can take anywhere from a few days to a couple of weeks.

Rinse the pork belly under cold running water, using your fingertips to scrub off any remaining sugar and salt. Pat dry with a rag. Hang in a protected area where air flows freely. We keep ours hanging from meat hooks above the kitchen counter.

MAPLE SODA BREAD WITH RAISINS

Serves 4

2 cups einkorn flour, or sprouted all-purpose flour of choice

1 teaspoon baking soda

1 teaspoon baking powder

½ teaspoon sea salt

½ cup raisins

1 lemon, zested

4 tablespoons butter, cut into small pieces, plus extra for greasing baking sheet

¾ cup buttermilk

3 tablespoons maple syrup

½ teaspoon vanilla

My husband has a thing for breads and this quick bread is one of his favorites. There is no limit to what can be tucked inside: dried fruits, chopped nuts, toasted coconut. Just don't expect the loaf to last for more than a few minutes—greedy hands and empty stomachs will find it quickly!

Preheat the oven to 325°F. Lightly grease a baking sheet with butter.

Combine the flour, baking soda, baking powder, and salt in a large bowl. Add the raisins and lemon zest and stir to combine. Add the butter pieces to the flour mixture, using your fingertips to integrate them together until the flour resembles coarse crumbs.

In a separate bowl, mix together the buttermilk, maple syrup, and vanilla and add to the flour mixture. Gently mix to combine. On a floured work surface, carefully and gently knead the dough together. Don't overdo it. Just knead to combine and shape into a disk, about 6 inches across and 2 inches thick.

Using a sharp knife, cut an X into the top of the bread, about ½-inch deep. Place the loaf directly onto the greased baking sheet and bake for 30 to 40 minutes, until golden.

SOURDOUGH SKILLET BREAD

Makes a 12-inch flat loaf

Sourdough bread is an art form that I've yet to master, but this is one sourdough recipe I can make. It utilizes the extra sourdough starter that one would normally discard. Enhanced with salt and some fresh herbs, it's a beauty to behold and oh-so-delicious with a few fried eggs.

Preheat the oven to 375°F.

Heat a 10- to 12-inch cast-iron skillet over medium-high heat, add the butter and olive oil, and allow to melt.

In a large bowl, whisk together the sourdough starter, baking soda, and sea salt. Pour the dough into the skillet and sprinkle with the rosemary and pine nuts. Allow the dough to cook for 3 to 4 minutes to set the bottom of the skillet bread, before removing from the stovetop and placing in the oven. Bake for 10 to 12 minutes, until gently puffed and golden.

Cut the skillet bread into wedges and drizzle with additional olive oil before serving.

1 teaspoon butter

1 teaspoon olive oil, plus extra for serving

1½ to 2 cups Sourdough Starter (see page 222)

¾ teaspoon baking soda

¾ teaspoon sea salt

1 teaspoon fresh rosemary

2 tablespoons pine nuts

BREAKFAST BROTH WITH POACHED EGGS

Serves 4

8 cups Chicken Stock
(see page 64)

Sea salt

Freshly ground black
pepper

8 eggs

Fresh herbs, minced, for
garnish

Pumpkin seeds, toasted,
for garnish

1 lemon wedge

Chicken broth for breakfast—say whaaaat? Though it's not common for us Westerners to sip on warm broth in the morning, each time I make this dish for breakfast, I'm surprised at how nourished I feel. Even my little ones love it. A gently poached egg and a few toasted seeds really bring the flavors to life.

In a large saucepan heat the stock over medium heat. Season with salt and pepper. Taste, season, taste again. Get it right—this is important!

When the stock is just barely simmering, quickly and carefully crack each egg directly into the broth. Allow the eggs to gently simmer for 2 to 3 minutes, until just set, but with the yolks still runny. Carefully scoop 2 eggs per serving into a bowl with a generous ladle of the chicken stock.

Garnish with a generous pinch of fresh herbs, toasted pumpkin seeds, and a squeeze of fresh lemon juice.

EINKORN PUFF PASTRY

Makes about 1 pound

2 cups all-purpose einkorn flour

½ teaspoon sea salt

½ cup filtered water

20 tablespoons unsalted butter, at room temperature, divided

Yes, you can buy puff pastry in the grocery store. But that wouldn't be nearly as fun or delicious, now would it? So here we are—the real deal. Let's use the best wheat. And the best butter. This is a simple and basic method for creating a rich and flaky pastry dough that's sure to blow your mind.

In a bowl, sift together the flour and salt. Add the water and 4 tablespoons of the butter. Use your fingers to gently work the dough into a ball. Wrap the ball in plastic wrap and stick in the refrigerator for 30 minutes while you go snuggle baby lambs. Or, focus on the next step.

Place a 12-inch sheet of parchment paper on your work surface. Place the remaining 16 tablespoons of butter on the parchment paper and cover with a second sheet of parchment. Using a rolling pin, shape the butter into a 5 × 8-inch rectangle. Place in the refrigerator for 30 minutes to chill slightly.

Remove the ball of dough from the refrigerator. Cut a large X into the top of the ball and pull each corner out, like you're opening a gift box! This will help you begin to shape the rectangle we're aiming for. Lightly flour your work surface and begin to gently roll the dough into a 10-inch square(ish) rectangle.

Place the flattened butter in the center of the flattened dough and fold in the corners. Roll out gently to combine the butter and the dough into a rectangle. Turn the dough so that a short side of the rectangle is facing you, then fold the dough into thirds, like an envelope. Gently roll this into a rectangle. Cover with plastic wrap and refrigerate for 30 minutes.

Remove the dough from the refrigerator, fold it into thirds again, and gently roll into an 8 x 12-inch rectangle. Cover with plastic wrap and refrigerate for 30 minutes. You know what we're doing here? We're building layers of flaky dough. Each time we fold and roll, we're creating a new layer of buttery awesomeness. Repeat the folding/rolling/chilling routine 5 more times.

The dough can be stored in the refrigerator for 3 days or in the freezer for up to 1 month! Bake according to any recipe that calls for puff pastry, such as tarts, popovers, or pasties.

BLUEBERRY, CHIA, AND MINT SMOOTHIE

Serves 4

Treat yo'self to this smoothie—you won't be disappointed. It'll send you into your day with pep in your step, that's for sure!

Blend the ingredients together in a high-powered blender until smooth. Pour into a chilled glass and garnish with fresh mint. Mmm!

6 cups frozen blueberries

½ cup vanilla yogurt, custard, or kefir

6 tablespoons chia seeds

¼ cup fresh mint

6 dates, or 2 tablespoons maple syrup, to taste

2 cups raw milk (or coconut milk)

BLUEBERRY AND BANANA BREAKFAST BAKE

Serves 6

3 large bananas, peeled and sliced

5–7 slices of thick-cut bread (such as French or artisan bread . . . something a bit sturdy)

8 eggs

3 cups whole milk

½ cup maple syrup or honey

2 teaspoons cinnamon

2 teaspoons vanilla extract

⅛ teaspoon ground nutmeg

Pinch of sea salt

1½ cups blueberries (fresh or frozen)

6 tablespoons butter

Maple syrup or honey, for serving

I always feel like a rock star when I make this dish, because my kids go crazy for it! It's not complicated, but apparently it has magic powers on children who wake up hungry from a good night's sleep. I'll take it.

Preheat the oven to 350°F.

Butter a 9 × 13-baking dish generously. Lay the bananas in a single layer on the bottom of the pan.

Cut the bread into 1-inch cubes. Layer the bread on top of the bananas.

Whip together the eggs, milk, maple syrup or honey, cinnamon, vanilla, nutmeg, and salt. Pour this mixture over the bread and bananas. Layer on the blueberries and then the butter, pinched into small pieces, over the top of the dish.

Bake for 40 minutes or until the top is golden and a bit crusty.

EINKORN MAPLE AND WALNUT LOAF

Makes 2 large loaves

1 recipe sourdough
levain (recipe below)

2½ cups warm water

6 cups whole grain
einkorn flour

6 cups all-purpose
einkorn flour

3 teaspoons sea salt

2 cups chopped walnuts

½ cup maple syrup

This is my very favorite einkorn bread. It's maple-sweetened and littered with chopped walnuts. It's hearty, easy, and so dang delicious.

The night before, mix together the sourdough levain. Let it sit out on the counter overnight.

The next morning, mix together the levain and water.

In a large bowl mix together the flours, salt, walnuts, and maple syrup. Pour the levain into the flour mixture. Mix to combine. Let the mixture sit for 15 minutes.

On a floured surface knead the dough until smooth, adding a bit more flour if necessary to keep the dough from sticking. Divide the dough in two. Roll each loaf into a ball, tucking the sides underneath the loaf to create a smooth surface. Place the loaves on a heavily floured kitchen towel and dust the top with flour. Cover with plastic wrap (or a kitchen towel) and let the loaves rise in a warm area for 3 to 5 hours.

Preheat a dutch oven in a 450°F oven. While the oven is preheating, gently squish the loaf into an oval before grabbing the sides of the oval and tucking them back into the middle. Flip the loaf over. You should have created a beautiful, smooth, round loaf. Let the loaves rest again for 60 to 90 minutes (plastic wrap over the top will prevent a premature crust from forming).

Place one of the loaves into the preheated dutch oven. Slash the top with a sharp knife in a hashtag pattern. Put the lid on and bake for 40 minutes. If you like a browner loaf, remove the lid and bake for 5 more minutes.

Remove the first loaf and repeat step 6 with the second loaf. Allow the loaves to cool on a wire rack before eating. If, unlike Stuart, you can wait that long.

SOURDOUGH LEVAIN

Combine the sourdough starter (inactive or active) with the water. Stir to combine.

Mix in the flour.

Let the levain sit at room temperature for 6 to 10 hours.

4 tablespoons Sourdough Starter (see page 222)

1 cup water

2 cups einkorn flour

VANILLA AND MAPLE BREAD PUDDING

Serves 6

A more sophisticated take on the Blueberry and Banana Breakfast Bake, this dish is one that always gets oohs and aahs from breakfast visitors. Shh . . . don't tell them I make it from stale bread.

Preheat the oven to 375°F.

Slice the bread into ½-inch cubes. You should end up with about 6 cups.

Butter a 12-inch cast-iron skillet (or baking dish of choice). Place the bread cubes in the skillet.

In a bowl, combine the butter, milk, eggs, cinnamon, salt, vanilla extract, and maple syrup. Whisk to combine. Pour the mixture over the bread cubes and use a fork to gently move the bread cubes around, allowing the sweet liquid to leak into all the cracks and crevices. Sprinkle the golden raisins and sliced almonds over the top.

Bake in the oven for 35 to 40 minutes, until the bread pudding is just set. You don't want it "set" set, but you don't want it too jiggly either, or you'll have bread soup. Just a gentle jiggle in the middle is all you need.

6 slices stale, crusty bread

⅓ cup melted butter

2 cups whole milk (or cream, no judgment)

4 eggs

2 teaspoons cinnamon

Large pinch of sea salt

1 tablespoon vanilla extract (or beans from 1 vanilla pod)

½ cup maple syrup

¾ cup golden raisins (or dried fruit of choice)

½ cup sliced almonds

Fresh Bread Day

Fresh bread day. The day when my children and husband linger around the kitchen for hours, sneaking bits of bread from the corners of the loaves. Oftentimes they'll nibble uncontrollably, thinking I won't notice the extra chunk taken from the piping-hot bread. But I do. And I let them, because there are few greater joys in the world, or at least on our farm, than fresh bread day.

Bread is measured, mixed, and shaped with my own hands. The basic ingredient list is simple, "rising" from a few different combinations of flour, water, yeast, and salt. It comes twice per week—often it's crunchy artisan loaves, though sometimes it's soaked whole wheat sandwich bread or sourdough. Regardless of the flour or leavening agent used, it's essential. Bread is fundamental to the functioning of our farm; I swear my husband can only make it for so long without that crunchy crust and soft, chewy interior. It's the perfect companion for a ripe tomato from the garden and a fantastic vehicle for homemade preserves.

There's a common misconception that bread baking is hard work, reserved for only the perfect stay-at-home mom who has nothing better to do than babysit a bowl of proofing dough all day. But that doesn't fly around here. My time for chores, even kitchen chores, is limited, so my bread baking has been adapted to fit such a schedule. Believe it or not, some of the best breads I bake are those that require the least amount of care or precision. This adaptation, and finding what styles of bread work best in our daily eating, is what makes it possible for fresh bread day to happen. Because the baking can require such a small amount of attention, it's possible to bring those warm loaves to the table meal after meal—much to my family's delight.

Fresh bread day, when those fragrant and rustic loaves make their appearance, sums up what is so enjoyable about this life. It's slowing down long enough to invest in a food that will feed our souls. It's working and creating with our hands. It's opening a jar of apricot jam and passing it around the table, each of us generously coating our slice of bread and licking the extra drips off our fingers. It's enjoying fleeting pleasures, like the perfect crunch of the bread crust just minutes out of the oven. It's opening our home to friends and breaking bread with our hands as we pass the loaves around the table.

Bread is community. Bread is life. Bread is, well, bread is delicious.

soups
and
salads

CHICKEN STOCK

Makes 1½ gallons

1 whole chicken

3 onions

3 stalks celery

3 carrots

20 whole black
   peppercorns

1 bunch parsley

1 cup vinegar

3-4 cleaned chicken
   feet, optional

1½ gallons filtered water

We're rarely found without a gigantic pot of chicken stock simmering on the stove, an absolute staple in our homestead kitchen. Homemade stock is rich in trace minerals and vitamins—feeding the body and the soul. It's a building block for many of the recipes in our kitchen and is quite often enjoyed on its own. It's like a nourishing poultry hug, in the best way possible.

Combine all of the ingredients together in a large stockpot. Allow to sit for 30 minutes so the vinegar can begin to draw the minerals from the chicken.

Bring the stock up to a very low simmer, cover, and allow it to remain on the gentlest simmer possible for 12 hours. *It shouldn't come to a rapidly boil at any point.* Just keep it hot and steaming.

Remove the stock from heat and allow to cool to room temperature. Strain the stock from the solids and refrigerate. The chicken can be picked of the meat, which can easily be used in a variety of recipes. The stock is best used up within a week or can be frozen for future use.

ROASTED SUNCHOKES WITH TOMATOES AND LEMON

Serves 4–6

We began growing sunchokes (also known as Jerusalem artichokes) a few years ago and quickly fell in love. If sunchokes aren't available at your local market, you can easily substitute with fingerling potatoes. This dish is perfect alongside a grilled steak and best enjoyed out in the garden during the summertime.

Preheat the oven to 425°F.

In a large bowl, combine the sunchokes, 4 tablespoons of the olive oil, generous pinches of the sea salt and black pepper, and the minced garlic. Toss to coat and spread evenly on a baking sheet. Bake in the oven for 30 minutes, or until golden and slightly crispy.

Return the sunchoke slices, and all the residual liquid from the baking sheet, to the large bowl. Add the lemon zest and juice, the remaining 3 tablespoons of olive oil, thyme leaves, and tomatoes. Gently toss to combine. Season with additional salt and pepper, as desired, and serve immediately.

1½ pounds fresh unpeeled sunchokes, cut into ½-inch slices

7 tablespoons extra-virgin olive oil, divided

Sea salt

Freshly ground black pepper

4 cloves garlic, minced

1 lemon, zested and juiced

2 sprigs fresh thyme, stemmed

½ pound cherry tomatoes, halved

CHOPPED APPLE SALAD WITH TOASTED COCONUT AND YOGURT

Serves 4

½ cup almonds

½ cup shredded unsweetened coconut

2 large apples, peeled

½ cup plain yogurt

1 tablespoon raw honey

1 teaspoon ground cinnamon, plus a little extra for garnish

½ lemon, juiced

A simple recipe to spice up the abundance of apples we seem to find ourselves with each autumn, this salad is always welcomed at the table.

In a small skillet, combine the almonds and coconut. Gently toast over low heat for 3 to 5 minutes, or until fragrant. Remove from heat and set aside.

While the almonds and coconut are toasting, peel, core, and roughly chop the apples into ½-inch pieces. When cool, roughly chop the toasted almond and coconut mixture and combine with the apples, yogurt, honey, cinnamon, and lemon juice in a large bowl. Mix to evenly coat. Garnish with more cinnamon, if desired.

SALMON CHOWDER WITH DILL AND CARAWAY

Serves 4–6

I like to think of this warming soup as one of our "fast food" staples. If I'm late on fixing supper, I almost always have what I need to quickly throw it together. Best served with a heavily buttered crusty bread—naturally.

Melt the butter in a large stockpot. Add the onion and carrots and sauté for 5 minutes, or until the onion is soft and translucent. Add the potatoes and garlic and sauté for 3 to 4 minutes more, until fragrant. Add the chicken stock, followed by the dill, caraway seeds, and red pepper flakes. Allow the soup to gently simmer for 20 minutes, stirring occasionally, or until the potatoes are fork-tender.

Add the cream and salmon, stir again, and then cover and let the chowder gently simmer for 10 to 15 minutes more. Season with salt and pepper. Garnish with additional fresh dill and a small spoonful of sour cream, if desired.

4 tablespoons butter

1 large onion, diced

2 cups shredded carrots

2 cups diced potatoes

2 cloves garlic, minced

6 cups Chicken Stock (see page 64)

Small pinch of fresh or dried dill, plus a little extra for garnish

Small pinch of caraway seeds

Small pinch of red pepper flakes

1½ cups cream

12 ounces wild-caught salmon, fresh or canned

Sea salt

Freshly ground black pepper

1 tablespoon sour cream (optional)

CREAMY CARROT SOUP

Serves 6–8

5 tablespoons butter

2 large onions, roughly chopped

1 teaspoon fresh thyme leaves

Sea salt

2½ pounds carrots, roughly chopped

6 cups vegetable or chicken broth (see page 64)

1 teaspoon raw apple cider vinegar

Sea salt

Freshly ground black pepper

Toasted sunflower and sesame seeds, for garnish

Freshly chopped parsley, for garnish

I have an unashamed love for carrots. They're so sweet! And when combined with a few basic ingredients, they really come to life in this creamy soup. My kids always lap up multiple servings.

Melt the butter in a large stockpot. Add the onions and sprinkle with the thyme and a generous pinch of the sea salt. Let the onions soften in the butter for 10 minutes. Add the carrots and cook with the onions for 10 to 15 minutes, until the carrots are fork-tender. A light golden coloring on the vegetables indicates caramelization and will add nice flavor, but be careful not to overbrown—this is a gently flavored soup. Add the broth and cider vinegar. Allow the soup to simmer for 30 minutes.

Using an immersion blender, thoroughly blend the soup to a smooth puree. Season with salt and pepper. Garnish with a sprinkling of toasted sunflower and sesame seeds and a pinch of freshly chopped parsley.

ASPARAGUS SOUP WITH POACHED EGGS

Serves 4

Around here asparagus often grows wild by the sides of the orchards and pastures. I am always eager and happy to see it arrive on the market tables each spring. Some I pickle, some we eat fresh, and even more I whirl into this soup.

In a dutch oven or stockpot, melt the butter. Once melted, add in the asparagus, onions, and celery. Gently soften the vegetables for 5 to 10 minutes. Don't brown or color them, just gently soften them; we want to keep all that delicious color!

Once the vegetables are softened, pour in the chicken stock.

Transfer the soup to a blender (or use an immersion blender). Blend the soup until it's perfectly smooth. Once the soup is smooth, return it once again to the dutch oven and gently heat it up over medium heat. Season to taste with sea salt and pepper. If the soup needs a bit of a pick-me-up, give it a nice squeeze of lemon juice; it's such a delicious complement to asparagus.

While the soup is heating up, poach one egg per serving. Serve the warm soup, topped with a poached egg and grated Parmesan cheese, and another sprinkling of sea salt and black pepper. Naturally, a wonderful crusty bread is the perfect accompaniment.

¼ cup butter

2 pounds fresh asparagus, woody stems removed

3 onions, peeled and roughly chopped

4 stalks celery, roughly chopped

8 cups chicken stock (see page 64) or vegetable stock

Sea salt

Freshly ground pepper to taste

Freshly squeezed lemon juice, to taste

4 poached eggs, for serving

Grated Parmesan cheese, for serving

Crusty bread, for serving

EASY BEET SOUP

Serves 4–6

1 tablespoon butter

1 onion, roughly
chopped

5 medium beets,
roughly chopped

Large pinch of sea
salt, plus extra for
seasoning

4 cups Chicken Stock
(see page 64)

1 teaspoon freshly
squeezed lemon juice

Freshly ground black
pepper

Roasted seeds, for
garnish

Crumbled feta cheese,
for garnish

Freshly chopped herbs,
for garnish

A favorite way to use up a surplus of garden beets, this quick-fix soup is what I turn to. Highlighted with toasted sunflower seeds, freshly chopped herbs, and a bit of feta cheese, it's winner-winner-beets-for-dinner.

Heat the butter in a dutch oven. Add the onion and beets and gently sauté for 10 minutes to get the flavors goin', yo. Add the salt and chicken stock. Bring to a simmer and cover. Let the soup simmer for 10 to 15 minutes, until the beets are very tender. Remove from the heat and, using an immersion blender, puree the soup until smooth. Add the lemon juice and season with salt and pepper. Dish up—garnishing each bowl with a healthy pinch of seeds, feta, and herbs.

TORTELLINI SOUP WITH CHICKEN AND PINE NUTS

Serves 4

I'm a sucker for pasta—a completely crazy-in-love sucker. I love that this dish highlights the tortellini without sitting quite as heavy in your belly as a traditional pasta dish does. Use whatever garden veggies you've got on hand!

Heat the olive oil in a large pot. Add the diced onion and sauté for 5 minutes, until soft and translucent. Add the garlic and chile and sauté for 2 minutes more, until fragrant. Add the bell peppers and tomatoes. Cook for 5 minutes, until the tomatoes begin to release their liquid. Add the pesto, chicken stock, cooked chicken, tortellini, and a large pinch or two of salt. Bring to a low simmer and cook until the tortellini are tender, about 15 minutes. Garnish with pine nuts, fresh thyme, and parsley and season with pepper, as desired.

3 tablespoons olive oil

2 onions, diced

6 garlic cloves, minced

1 red chile, minced, or ½ teaspoon dried chile flakes

2 cups diced red, yellow, or orange bell peppers

3 cups cherry tomatoes or diced tomatoes

2 tablespoons Basil Pesto (see page 218)

4 cups Chicken Stock (see page 64)

2 cups cooked chicken (leftover roast chicken works wonderfully)

1 cup tortellini (fresh and organic is best)

Sea salt

Pine nuts, for garnish

Fresh thyme, for garnish

Fresh parsley, for garnish

Freshly ground black pepper

CARROT SALAD

Serves 4–6

1 pound carrots, very thinly sliced

¼ cup almonds, toasted and chopped

3 tablespoons minced cilantro, plus extra for garnish

4 tablespoons crumbled feta or goat cheese, plus extra for garnish

2 tablespoons olive oil

1 tablespoon honey

3 tablespoons raw apple cider vinegar

Sea salt

Freshly ground black pepper

Yet another way to utilize a bumper crop of carrots, this is a flavorful, easy, and deliciously crunchy salad. I told you: My love for carrots has no bounds.

Place the sliced carrots in a serving bowl and top with the almonds, cilantro, and feta.

In a separate bowl, whisk together the olive oil, honey, and cider vinegar. Drizzle the dressing over the salad and gently toss to coat. Take a bite and then season with salt and pepper to taste. Garnish with additional feta and cilantro before serving.

SESAME-CRUSTED ORANGE CHICKEN SALAD

Serves 4

The word salad doesn't really do this dish justice. Frankly, it's a chickeny-orange masterpiece. I like it best with kale and spinach, but use whatever greens you've got on hand.

In a bowl, combine the sesame seeds, orange zest, and salt and pepper to taste. Place the chicken thighs, one at a time, into the sesame-orange mixture, turning to completely coat each piece.

Heat the butter and olive oil in a large skillet. Transfer the coated chicken thighs to the warm skillet and gently cook for 5 to 6 minutes on one side, turn, and cook 2 to 3 minutes on the other side, until cooked thoroughly and golden. Remove from the skillet and set aside to rest.

Plate the salads by dividing the fresh greens evenly and arranging them among four plates. Top the greens with the bell pepper slices, grated carrots, and a few tablespoons of feta. Slice the chicken thighs into ½-inch strips and place them atop the salads.

In a bowl, blend or whisk the dressing ingredients together until smooth and drizzle over each of the salads.

For the salad:
¾ cup sesame seeds

1 orange, zested

Sea salt

Freshly ground black pepper

1½ pounds chicken thighs

2 tablespoons butter

2 tablespoons olive oil

1½ pounds fresh greens, such as lettuce, spinach, and kale

1 red bell pepper, sliced into thin rings

3 carrots, grated

8 tablespoons feta cheese

For the dressing:
3 tablespoons olive oil

2 oranges, zested and juiced

½-inch piece fresh ginger, minced

1 tablespoon honey

CREAMY LEEK AND CHICKPEA STEW

Serves 4–6

3 leeks, roughly
chopped

4 tablespoons butter

1 onion, roughly
chopped

2 carrots, roughly
chopped

1 sweet potato, roughly
chopped

Sea salt

3 cups filtered water

Freshly ground black
pepper

1½ cups cooked
chickpeas

Cilantro, minced

1 red bell pepper,
minced

Sour cream

Another wonderful way to highlight vegetables in your little ones' diets, this hearty stew nourishes their guts and their appetites. Top with whatever garnishes you wish. My favorites are sour cream, chopped bell pepper, and fresh cilantro.

Fill a large bowl with water and add the chopped leeks. This allows the sand and dirt that sneak into the leeks to be released to the bottom of the bowl.

While the leeks are soaking, melt the butter in a large saucepan. When melted, add the leeks, onion, carrots, sweet potato, and a large pinch of sea salt. Allow the vegetables to soften for 20 minutes, until fork-tender. Keep an eye on the vegetables to avoid letting them brown too much—this is a rustic stew, but we want to keep the flavors clean.

When the vegetables are softened, spoon them into a high-powered blender and add 3 cups filtered water. Blend thoroughly until completely smooth. Transfer back to the saucepan and place over low heat. Season with salt and pepper. Add the chickpeas and gently warm until heated through.

Serve in bowls, topped with freshly chopped cilantro, bell pepper, and a dollop of sour cream.

CHOPPED SALAD WITH CHIVE CREAM

Serves 4

When you grow your own produce, or source it from high-quality growers, you'll enjoy salads like you've never enjoyed them before. Instead of being bland, each ingredient sings with flavor—sings, I tell you! As always, use what you've got on hand. Different meats, cheeses, or vegetables are welcome additions.

Arrange the greens among four plates. Divide the bacon evenly and arrange on the greens. Place an avocado half, peeled and sliced, atop each salad. Divide the feta evenly and sprinkle over each salad. Add 2 hard-boiled eggs to each serving and add a few sliced radishes as well, for some extra crunch. Ladies and gentlemen, meet your salad base.

Combine the honey, sour cream, cider vinegar, chives, and miso in a high-powered blender and blend on medium speed. Slowly drizzle in the olive oil until the chive cream is thick and completely combined. Season with salt and pepper, to taste. Add a heaping tablespoon of the dressing over each salad. Garnish with additional salt, pepper, or chives, as desired.

For the salad:

- 8 cups mixed greens, such as kale, mustard, collards, chard, or lettuce
- 8 slices bacon, fried and crumbled
- 2 avocados, halved
- 4 tablespoons feta cheese
- 8 eggs, hard-boiled and peeled
- 12 radishes, sliced

For the chive cream:

- 1 tablespoon honey
- 2 tablespoons sour cream
- 2 tablespoons raw apple cider vinegar
- 2 tablespoons fresh chives, plus extra for garnish
- 1 teaspoon miso paste
- ¾ cup extra-virgin olive oil
- Sea salt
- Freshly ground black pepper

CUCUMBER SALAD WITH MINT

Serves 6

1½ pounds cucumbers

1 lemon, juiced

3 tablespoons olive oil

½ cup heavy cream

Sea salt

Freshly ground black pepper

¼ cup minced fresh mint leaves

This is one summer salad that is not dressed in mayonnaise (as so many of them are), and it uses up extra cucumbers from the garden. It's great on its own as a side salad or is easily enjoyed atop meat or in sandwiches. Win-win, baby.

Cut the cucumbers in half lengthwise. Use a spoon to scoop out the seedy middle. This is, of course, an optional step, but by removing the seeds, we're not only improving the texture of the salad, we're also taking a lot of the liquid out so it doesn't become cucumber soup. I don't bother peeling my cucumbers because they have a very crispy thin skin, but if yours are thick or bitter, feel free to peel.

Cut the cucumbers into thin slices, widthwise, and place into a serving bowl.

In a separate small bowl, whisk together the lemon juice, olive oil, and cream and drizzle over the cucumbers. Season with salt and pepper.

Allow the cucumbers to marinate in the dressing for a bit. It gives the flavors time to marry. And married flavors are tasty flavors.

Before serving, add the mint leaves and gently toss. Add an extra grinding or two of fresh pepper—because it looks pretty, that's why. So do it! Sorry. I don't mean to be bossy. But I like pretty dishes, which is part of the reason why I love this easy salad. The little flecks of bright green mint totally make me swoon. Enjoy!

Will Work for Salad

There is hardly a task I love more on the farm than tending the vegetable garden. As ruby-red tomatoes begin to weigh down their branches in mid-July, life is at its sweetest. Firm, deep-purple eggplant drip from their silver leaves; onions poke their tall greens from the ground; carrots begin to fluff out their feathery tops; chard is as vibrant as a rainbow; basil, rosemary, chives, and oregano are invigorating the entire landscape with their smell; and beets are boldly pushing their dark-red heads from the soil. It's the most magnificent show one could imagine.

I think it's the natural beauty that draws me back year after year to the toil of the garden. In mid-February, when I first begin my indoor seed planting, I eagerly anticipate another year spent with my fingers dug into that cool garden soil. And by mid-April, my back is usually cursing whoever thought planting such a large garden was a good idea.

But then the lettuce comes. And shortly thereafter, the peas and the asparagus. We'll enjoy them cooked in a bit of homemade butter and topped with a poached spring egg from the hens. Pretty soon we can once again snip the fresh herbs and perhaps even snag a few kale leaves if we're lucky.

Each vegetable harvested from the garden is a reminder of why it is we go to such great effort to fill our garden beds each year. The taste. The flavor. The colors. The texture. The freshness. It's without comparison. Truly, a thriving vegetable garden makes one feel like a king.

And so we toil, day after day, night after night, in our wonderful gardens, planting potato seeds, harvesting garlic, or spreading thick layers of hay mulch between the crooked rows.

It's the most beautiful, and most delicious, work one could ever be a part of.

side
dishes

TRADITIONAL RATATOUILLE

Serves 6

¼ cup good olive oil

Sprigs of fresh thyme

3 bay leaves

3 garlic cloves

2 yellow onions

4 bell peppers, diced

3 medium eggplant, diced

2 medium zucchini, diced

4 large tomatoes, seeded and diced

Sea salt and pepper, to taste

Each summer, when the sun heats up the garden bed and the vegetables begin to ripen, ratatouille is the very first dish on my to-make list. Year upon year, I spend July, August, and September gorging myself on the very best summer vegetables the garden has to offer, and most of the time, it's in the form of this traditional ratatouille recipe.

Heat a medium-size cast-iron skillet. Add the olive oil, thyme, and bay leaves. Crush the garlic, remove the skins, and add the whole cloves to the skillet. This is our base of ingredients that we will keep in there the entire time.

Over medium heat, sauté the onion in the olive oil, garlic, and herbs until just soft. Leave it with the teeniest bit of crunch. Remove the onion to a plate, reserving the thyme, bay leaves, and garlic in the pan.

Toss the peppers into the skillet. Add a bit more olive oil, if need be, to keep it all moist and sauté-like. Remove the peppers while they're still slightly crunchy and place atop the onions, reserving the thyme, bay leaves, and garlic in the pan . . . once again. Are you catching on to the pattern that we're only cooking one vegetable at a time? It all has to do with the texture of the ratatouille. Each vegetable cooks at a different rate, so this method ensures the entire dish is cooked perfectly. If this isn't your style, feel free to throw it all in together. It's your ratatouille, after all.

Next, add the eggplant to the skillet. Eggplant has a tendency to soak up the olive oil, so add a bit more if need be. Don't overcook the eggplant! Ain't nobody like overcooked eggplant. Remove the eggplant to the plate and then add the zucchini.

And lastly, add the tomatoes to the skillet, but not before you've seeded them. Tomatoes with seeds will make the ratatouille soggy, and ratatouille should not be soggy. My superfancy method of seeding tomatoes is to cut the tomato in half before sticking my thumb into the squishy center and squeezing the seeds out over my compost bucket. Sauté until the tomatoes are slightly cooked. Spoon onto the rest of the vegetables, omitting the thyme stems and garlic cloves.

Did you know that *ratatouille* comes from the French verb *touiller*, which means "to stir up"? Let's gently stir to bring it all together, shall we? Then you can add salt and pepper to taste.

HOMEMADE CHORIZO

Makes 3 pounds

We raise pigs each year, and it's for two reasons: bacon and chorizo. This is an excellent meat to crisp up in a skillet and sprinkle on potatoes, rice, salad, sautéed vegetables, or even your morning eggs. It's rich, so a little goes a long way. Chorizo, like sausage, can be enjoyed a zillion different ways. Breakfast, lunch, or dinner. Eggs, soups, salads, casseroles. You name it. Throw in a few small potatoes to cook alongside the chorizo, toss in some greens and radishes right before serving. And that's it. Culinary salvation in a skillet.

Put the ground pork in a large bowl. Set aside. Ignore the pork. Let the pork be.

Combine the onion, vinegar, cumin, coriander, bay leaves, cloves, allspice berries, cinnamon, oregano, parsley, salt, chile, pepper, paprikas, and garlic together in a food processor or high-powered blender.

Blend the ingredients until smooth, adding red wine as necessary to ensure it all gets blended well together. I just add the wine through the hole at the top of the blender until there's enough liquid in the mixture to really make it blended.

Combine the sauce and pork with your hands until well combined.

Oh, by the way, that's it! You've now made chorizo. All that's left is to fry it up. I do this on high heat, because I love it when the chorizo gets little crispy, browned bits.

---

3 pounds ground pork, at least 30 percent fat (aka: sausage meat)

1 large onion

3 tablespoons balsamic vinegar

1 tablespoon cumin

1 tablespoon coriander

3 bay leaves

5 cloves

2 allspice berries

¼ teaspoon cinnamon

1 tablespoon fresh oregano

1 tablespoon fresh parsley

1 teaspoon salt

½ teaspoon chili powder (or ½ teaspoon red pepper flakes)

½ teaspoon black pepper

1 tablespoon sweet paprika

1 tablespoon smoked paprika

5 cloves garlic

Red wine

BRUSCHETTA

Serves 4–6, depending on the size of the bread loaf

2 pounds garden tomatoes

6 tablespoons olive oil

Sea salt

Freshly ground black pepper

½ cup chopped fresh basil

Crusty bread slices, for serving

1 clove garlic

Balsamic vinegar

I'll never forget the first time I had bruschetta. I was a lifetime tomato hater and pregnant with my first child. While at a friend's house, I decided to partake of their homemade bruschetta. And my life was never, ever, ever the same. Quality makes all the difference in this dish—if you're not growing your own in a garden, splurge on the freshest, off-the-vine tomatoes you can find!

Gently chop the tomatoes into small pieces. I like to slice them all in one direction first, then carefully slice them in the opposite direction, so I end up with pretty squares. Drizzle with the olive oil. Add a small pinch of sea salt and freshly ground black pepper, to taste. Add the basil and stir to combine.

Place some thick bread slices under the broiler or into the toaster for a few minutes. Once the bread is nicely toasted, gently rub each slice with the garlic clove. Transfer the toasted garlic bread to a serving dish and drizzle generously with the balsamic vinegar. Top each slice of bread with a big ol' pile of the tomato mix and dig in!

CREAM CHEESE AND CHIVE POTATOES

Serves 4– 6

These potatoes are creamy, slightly smashed, and gently seasoned with chives. I'll take a big bowl of "Yes, please!" I won't even judge you for crumbling bacon over the top.

Heat the butter in a skillet over medium heat. When melted, add the potatoes, cover, and gently cook until they're fork-tender, about 15 minutes. Add the cream cheese and generous pinches of salt and pepper. Smash the potatoes and cream cheese together with a potato masher or fork until they're mostly creamy and combined, with just a few small potato pieces remaining for a little texture. Top with the chives and gently stir to incorporate just before serving.

4 tablespoons butter

2 pounds potatoes, cut into 1-inch pieces, skins on

⅓ cup cream cheese

Sea salt

Freshly ground black pepper

4 tablespoons minced chives

FROM-SCRATCH CORNBREAD

Serves 4

1 cup organic cornmeal

1 cup einkorn flour

½ teaspoon sea salt

3 teaspoons baking powder

1 tablespoon maple syrup

1 egg

1 cup milk

⅓ cup melted butter

Hey you, I see you making cornbread from a box. Ain't no shame in it! But next time, try this recipe. It takes almost no further effort on your part, and the taste is sublime enough to even make my Southern-born man sing its praises. If you don't have einkorn flour, you can easily substitute in another flour of your choosing. The recipe can also be doubled, or tripled.

Preheat the oven to 425°F.

Combine the cornmeal, flour, sea salt, and baking powder together in a bowl.

In a separate bowl, combine the maple syrup, egg, milk, and melted butter. Pour the liquid ingredients into the dry ingredients and gently whisk to combine. But don't overmix, baby.

Pour batter into a greased 8-inch pan and bake for 18 to 20 minutes, until golden and gently browned on the top.

ROASTED PEPPERS WITH BREAD, CHEESE, AND HERBS

Serves 4

Light up the grill so you can enjoy that delicious charred taste on your roasted sweet peppers. It makes them that much better.

Preheat oven to 475°F.

When I prepare the peppers, I like to cut them in half so that a bit of stem remains on each side, because I think it looks pretty.

In a bowl, use a fork to mix the cheese, bread crumbs, herbs, and red pepper flakes or diced red chile together. Salt and pepper to taste.

Lay the peppers on a baking sheet before stuffing each one with a bit of the mixture. Drizzle the peppers with a bit of olive oil before placing in the oven for 5 to 10 minutes, until roasted (but not too soft!), or light up the grill and roast until warm and toasty.

8 medium sweet peppers, cut in half and seeded

1 cup goat or crumbly cheese of choice

1 cup crusty bread, cut into teeny, tiny pieces or ground into crumbs

1 tablespoon minced chives

1 tablespoon minced rosemary

1 tablespoon fresh thyme leaves (lemon thyme is extra delicious)

Pinch of red pepper flakes or ¼ teaspoon diced red chile pepper

Salt

Freshly ground pepper

Olive oil

MUSHROOMS AND CREAM

Serves 4

2 tablespoons butter

5 cups mixed
   mushrooms

1 small onion, peeled
   and sliced into thin
   strips

Zest of 1 lemon

Juice of ½ lemon

½ cup heavy cream

Sea salt, to taste

Pepper, to taste

Loaf of crusty bread

Chopped parsley, to
   garnish

An absolutely delight served alongside a loaf of crusty bread, this skillet of mushrooms and cream—paired with a dry white wine—is all you need to fill your belly and spirits.

Melt the butter in a cast-iron skillet over medium heat. Add the mushrooms and onion and cook for 10 minutes, or until the mushrooms and onion begin to lightly brown and caramelize.

Add the lemon zest, lemon juice, cream, and a pinch of salt and pepper. Mix together with a spoon.

Bring the mixture to a boil before turning off the heat. Let the skillet rest for a few minutes while you slice up that crusty bread.

Garnish the mushrooms with parsley before serving. This dish is best eaten right out of the skillet, using the bread chunks to soak up all that delicious cream.

RUSTIC ROOT VEGETABLES WITH MISO VINAIGRETTE

Serves 4–6

Root vegetables have a special place in my heart and garden. Every year they faithfully see us through each winter. I love the brightness and tang that the vinaigrette adds to the vegetables' sweet and mellow flavors. Wake up, taste buds!

Preheat the oven to 375°F.

Roughly chop the root vegetables into 2-inch pieces. In a large baking dish, combine the root vegetables with the tomatoes and chicken stock. Season generously with salt and pepper. Roast in the oven for 40 minutes, or until the vegetables are nicely colored and tender.

While the vegetables roast, prepare the vinaigrette. In a food processor or blender, combine all the ingredients and blend until smooth. Set aside until needed.

When the vegetables are tender, pour the vinaigrette over all and continue roasting for another 10 to 15 minutes until golden.

For the vegetables:
3 pounds assorted root vegetables, such as potatoes, carrots, beets, onions, and parsnips

¼ pound fresh tomatoes, roughly chopped

1 cup Chicken Stock (see page 64)

Sea salt

Freshly ground black pepper

For the vinaigrette:
1 small shallot

1 tablespoon miso paste, or grainy mustard

1 tablespoon honey

⅔ cup olive oil

½ cup raw apple cider vinegar

HERBED ITALIAN FRIES

Serves 4–6

1 cup lard or tallow

2 pounds potatoes (any kind), cut into large wedges, skins on

3 large garlic cloves, minced

2 sprigs fresh thyme

2 sprigs fresh rosemary

Sea salt

Fresh parsley, chopped, for garnish

If there's anything better than potatoes fried in lard, I've yet to discover what it is. A cast-iron skillet will serve you well for this dish—it holds a high heat and helps you achieve that delicious crust we're going for.

Heat the lard or tallow in a large cast-iron skillet until it begins to barely smoke. Carefully add the potatoes—use a large spoon rather than just dumping them in, so as not to accidentally splash yourself with hot oil! Gently maneuver the potatoes around the skillet so they are in a single layer. Cook for 4 to 6 minutes, or until the potatoes turn a deep-golden color. Using tongs, flip the fries and cook for 2 to 3 minutes more, until deeply golden on the other side. In the last 10 seconds of cooking, add the garlic, thyme, and rosemary. Be careful—they tend to make the oil spit! After 10 seconds, remove the herbs and garlic and set aside.

Transfer the fries to a serving plate lined with a tea towel. Instantly top the fries with a generous pinch of salt. Quickly strip the thyme and rosemary leaves from their stems and sprinkle the fried herbs over the fries.

Garnish with the fresh parsley and serve immediately.

ROASTED ONIONS

Serves 4

I know onions may not sound like the most exciting side dish ever, but—Lawd have mercy—these are delicious! They're a great accompaniment for grilled steak, roast chicken, or even just a good loaf of crusty bread.

Preheat the oven to 400°F.

Slice the onions into medium strips. I do this by cutting each onion in half from the top to bottom. I lay each half flat on the counter, then cut straight slices through the onion, again from top to bottom. Arrange the onions in a shallow baking dish or pie plate.

In a small bowl, whisk together the olive oil, honey, vinegar, salt, rosemary, and thyme. Drizzle the dressing over the onions. Roast in the oven for 30 to 40 minutes, until the onions are soft and sweet.

3 red onions

4 tablespoons olive oil

2 tablespoons honey

2 tablespoons mild vinegar, such as red wine vinegar

Pinch sea salt

Pinch dried rosemary

Pinch dried thyme

BRUSSELS SPROUTS GRATIN WITH BACON AND CREAM

Serves 4–6

1 pound brussels sprouts, cut in half

Sea salt

Filtered water

3 slices bacon

⅓ cup heavy cream

½ cup breadcrumbs

Olive oil

Freshly ground black pepper

Have you ever grown brussels sprouts? They take forever to grow. F-O-R-E-V-E-R. When they do finally come out, late in the fall, I can barely stand to let them finish growing. As soon as I can, I pluck them off and mix them with cream and bacon. Because, y'know, cream and bacon.

Place the brussels sprouts and a generous pinch of sea salt in a saucepan with enough filtered water to cover. Simmer until just barely fork-tender, about 10 minutes.

While the brussels sprouts are simmering, fry the bacon in a cast-iron skillet. When crispy but not brittle, remove the bacon from the skillet using a slotted spoon and chop into small pieces.

Preheat the oven to 425°F.

When the brussels sprouts are just tender, strain them from the hot water and transfer to a medium baking dish. Sprinkle the chopped bacon over the top. Pour the heavy cream over the sprouts and bacon. Lastly, sprinkle the breadcrumbs over the top. Drizzle generously with olive oil and add a few grinds of pepper. Bake in the oven until golden, about 10 minutes.

SPAGHETTI WITH PARSLEY AND GARLIC

Serves 4–6

This recipe is so basic, yet always so satisfying. Pair it with a nice glass of red wine and you'll never even miss the meat.

Bring a large pot of salted water to a boil. Add the pasta and cook until al dente.

While the pasta is cooking, heat the olive oil in a small saucepan. When the oil is just warm, add the garlic and sauté for 3 to 5 minutes, until just soft. The trick is not to brown the garlic, just gently soften it. For the last minute of cooking, add the parsley and chile flakes.

Drain the pasta, reserving ¼ cup of the cooking liquid. Transfer the pasta and reserved cooking liquid to a large serving bowl. Drizzle with the garlic–oil mixture and toss to combine. Season with salt and pepper and garnish with additional fresh parsley.

1 pound spaghetti, freshly made is best, but dried will do

½ cup olive oil

4 cloves garlic, minced

⅛ cup chopped fresh parsley, plus a little extra for garnish

¼ teaspoon red chile flakes

Sea salt

Freshly ground black pepper

PERFECT BROWNED BUTTER MASHED POTATOES

Serves 4–6

2 pounds russet potatoes, peeled and cut into 1-inch pieces

Filtered water

8 tablespoons butter

1 cup cream, room temperature

Sea salt

Freshly ground black pepper

Potatoes and butter? Yes. Potatoes and browned butter? Oh, heck yes.

Place the potatoes in a large saucepan with enough filtered water to cover by 1 inch, and boil until fork-tender, about 10 minutes.

While the potatoes are boiling, melt the butter in a small saucepan over medium heat. When the butter is melted, allow it to continue cooking until it begins to change color, which will continue to deepen the longer it remains over the heat. For this recipe, despite its title, we aren't going for brown, we're shooting for a light-golden color. When the butter reaches this shade, remove the pan from the heat and set aside.

When the potatoes are tender, drain in a colander before returning them to the saucepan. Mash the potatoes with a ricer, potato masher, or fork until your preferred consistency is reached. (I like mine to have a few chunks for texture.) Pour the golden-brown butter over the potatoes and gently fold in. Fold in the cream. Season with salt and pepper.

OVEN-FRIED ZUCCHINI WITH CILANTRO AIOLI

Serves 4

Fresh zucchini is a homestead staple, and this recipe turns a wonderfully crisp vegetable into something totally brilliant, if I do say so myself. By all means, use whatever vegetables you have on hand. We often do green tomatoes, eggplant, peppers, and even carrots.

Preheat the oven to 450°F. Drizzle a baking sheet with olive oil and place it in the oven to warm.

In a bowl, combine the ground almonds and Parmesan cheese.

In a separate bowl, whisk the eggs.

In a third bowl, place the flour.

Working with a few zucchini pieces at a time, add them first to the flour to coat and shake off any excess. Then dunk them into the eggs. Finally, dredge them in the almond–Parmesan mixture.

Remove the baking sheet from the oven and place the zucchini slices onto the oiled sheet. Season with salt and pepper and bake for 10 to 15 minutes, flipping them over halfway through the cooking time and adding salt and pepper to the other side. When golden, remove from the oven and transfer to a plate and serve with Cilantro Aioli.

2 tablespoons olive oil

1 cup ground almonds

1 cup grated Parmesan cheese

3 eggs

½ cup organic flour

3 zucchini, cut into ¼-inch slices

Sea salt

Freshly ground black pepper

1 recipe Cilantro Aioli (see page 217)

ROASTED GARLIC SCAPES

Serves 46

20–30 fresh garlic
  scapes

3 tablespoons olive oil

½ cup freshly grated
  Parmesan cheese

Sea salt

Freshly ground black
  pepper

Each year I look forward to our garlic bulbs sending up their shoots in the early spring. As they begin to develop, they grow these beautiful, curly scapes. With a mild garlicky flavor and a vibrant texture, they're a seasonal treat that's worth introducing to your family. If you don't grow garlic, ask around at your local farmers' market in the late spring and early summer.

Preheat the oven to 375°F.

Line a baking sheet with parchment paper and arrange the garlic scapes evenly across. Drizzle with the olive oil. Sprinkle with the shredded cheese and season with a little salt and pepper. Parmesan tends to be a salty cheese, so don't overdo it at first. Not that I've ever done this. Ahem.

Roast the scapes in the oven for 20 to 30 minutes. The goal is to prepare slightly softened and roasted scapes, not sad, mushy, and overcooked ones. That being said, roasting brings out the scapes' natural sweetness, so be sure to let them get to that delicious point.

The Fellowship of Self-Sufficiency

Homesteading is often equated with self-sufficiency. That we want to labor in this soil because we want to be able to do it all ourselves. For our farm, that's not exactly the case. Though I do delight in being able to provide much of what our family needs, the reality is, that's still far from the truth.

Our pigs and chickens are fed grain that we source from a local organic grower. He's older now, but is still keen to supply home-steaders like us with high-quality, bulk grain at a deep discount from the feed stores. We rely on his crops to grow and his machinery to work to provide us with what we need.

Our fruit trees and vegetable garden are productive, but they're still not near enough to provide us with a year-round supply of

produce, so we rely on farmer friends down the road who have much more land, and much more experience, than we do. We'll raise them a pig and in return, they'll share their bounty of cherries, pears, apples, plums, apricots, berries, and whatever vegetable odds and ends we aren't growing that season. We rely on them to help fill in the gaps.

Our pasture hadn't been used in more than thirty years prior to our arrival, and though the fences are up, the grass is still weak. While we work on the health of our pasture land, we rely on hay growers nearby to supply us with the high-quality forage our animals need to get through the fall and winter. We rely on their soil, the rain, and lots of machinery to fill our hay barn each summer.

I don't see this reliance as a weakness; rather I see it as a great strength. The richness that comes from supporting one another in this work is far stronger, and greater, than what any of us could achieve on our own. We've woven a net in our community that supports all of our lifestyles, pocketbooks, and health. We've gone beyond ourselves, and lifted others up where they can shine.

That's some delicious fellowship.

main dishes

BROWNED CHICKEN THIGHS WITH FINGERLING POTATOES AND CHERRY TOMATOES

Serves 4

2 pounds fingerling potatoes

Filtered water

8 boneless chicken thighs, preferably from organic, pastured poultry

2 tablespoons olive oil

Sea salt

Freshly ground black pepper

1½ pounds cherry tomatoes

Boiling water, to cover tomatoes

¼ cup fresh oregano, plus a little extra for garnish

3 tablespoons olive oil

2 tablespoons raw apple cider vinegar

During the summer months, when cherry tomatoes are at their peak, I make this dish more than I care to admit. In the winter I often utilize sun-dried or preserved cherry tomatoes and wouldn't y'know, it's just as delicious!

Place the potatoes in a medium pot with enough filtered water to cover. Boil until fork-tender, drain, and set aside.

While the potatoes are boiling, cut each chicken thigh into 3 strips. Place the chicken pieces into a large bowl. Drizzle with the olive oil and add a few generous pinches of sea salt and some freshly ground black pepper. (Yes, freshly ground black pepper matters. At least to me.) Use your hands to toss the chicken and coat it evenly with the oil, salt, and pepper. Transfer the chicken to a large cast-iron skillet, dutch oven, or large baking dish of choice.

Preheat the oven to 400°F.

Using a small sharp knife, puncture each cherry tomato and place in a small bowl. Cover with boiling water and allow the tomatoes to sit for 1 minute. Drain the hot water and carefully pinch the skin off each tomato. Add the drained potatoes and skinned tomatoes to the chicken.

Combine the oregano, olive oil, and cider vinegar in a blender or food processor. Blend until just combined, about 15 seconds. Pour the oregano oil over the chicken. Bake in the oven for 45 minutes, or until just gently browned on top. Garnish with sea salt, fresh pepper, and oregano.

ROASTED PORK SHOULDER

Serves 4–6

Pork shoulder is often ground into sausage because it tends to be slightly tough—after all, this is a muscle that the pig uses quite often. An alternative to grinding the shoulder cuts is to slow-roast them. Low 'n' slow in the oven renders the roast tender and succulent. It takes a wee bit of forethought to marinade and slow-roast, but it's absolutely worth it—especially when you bust out that moist, delicious roast for your friends. It's a par-tay!

Place the pork in a roasting pan. Sprinkle the pork with the sugar, vinegar, salt, pepper, olive oil, oregano, and cumin. Add the garlic cloves and lemon juice. Marinate for 6 hours in the refrigerator, turning the roast every few hours and spooning some of the marinade over the top.

Preheat the oven to 325°F.

Place the pork in the oven for 3½ hours, or until the internal temperature of the meat reaches 190°F. Remove from the oven and let rest for 10 to 15 minutes before slicing.

To serve, slice off thin slabs of roast and pour a spoonful of the cooking liquid over the top. Serve with rice, noodles, or roasted potatoes.

1 (2-pound) pork shoulder roast

2 tablespoons dehydrated whole cane sugar

2 tablespoons red wine vinegar

2 tablespoons sea salt

2 tablespoons freshly ground black pepper

1 tablespoon olive oil

2 teaspoons dried oregano

2 teaspoons dried cumin

10 cloves garlic

2 lemons, juiced

PAPRIKA AND ROSEMARY ROASTED CHICKEN

Serves 4

1 whole chicken, cut into 8 pieces (legs, thighs, wings, and breasts)

1 tablespoon tallow or olive oil

2 tablespoons all-purpose flour

2 tablespoons sweet paprika

1 teaspoon sea salt

1 teaspoon freshly ground black pepper

½ teaspoon cayenne pepper

1½ cups Chicken Stock (see page 64)

½ cup raw apple cider vinegar

12 cloves garlic

Fresh sprigs rosemary

Generously browned chicken pieces, seasoned, then simmered in a light sauce of stock, garlic, and vinegar—this is an extraordinary dish for an everyday meal!

Place the chicken pieces on a plate and, using a towel, pat the chicken dry. Excess liquid or water on the skin causes the chicken to boil rather than sear, which is what we're going for here. So pat away.

Heat the tallow in a large cast-iron skillet.

Combine the flour, paprika, sea salt, pepper, and cayenne in a bowl, stirring to mix. Place 1 chicken piece into the mixture and gently toss to coat. Set aside. Repeat with the remaining chicken pieces.

Add the chicken, a few pieces at a time, to the skillet (so as not to crowd them). Brown the chicken for 3 to 4 minutes per side, or until crusty and golden. When all the chicken pieces are browned, place them in a single layer in a large ungreased baking dish.

Preheat the oven to 350°F.

In a bowl, combine the chicken stock and vinegar and carefully pour into the hot skillet. Deglaze the skillet using a wooden spoon to stir and scrape up all the bits of seasoning and chicken left on the bottom. Allow the vinegar and broth to simmer for 5 minutes, or until slightly reduced. Pour over the chicken.

To the baking dish, add the garlic cloves and a few sprigs of the fresh rosemary. Bake in the oven for 30 minutes or until cooked thoroughly. Season with salt and pepper and garnish with the remaining rosemary.

SHREDDED BARBECUE BEEF SANDWICHES

Serves 6 to 8

- 1 (3- to 4-pound) beef roast, chuck or shoulder
- 2 teaspoons sea salt, divided
- 1 teaspoon freshly ground black pepper
- 3 teaspoons sweet paprika, divided
- 1 teaspoon olive oil
- 1 onion, minced
- 3 cloves garlic, minced
- ½ teaspoon red pepper flakes
- 6 cups fresh tomatoes, diced, or 1 (28-ounce) can diced tomatoes
- 4 tablespoons organic tomato paste
- ½ cup raw apple cider vinegar
- ⅓ cup molasses
- 1 tablespoon dehydrated cane sugar or maple syrup
- 1 tablespoon high-quality mustard
- 6 to 8 buns
- Shredded cabbage or sauerkraut, for texture

There's hardly a supper or lunch more satisfying than these beef sandwiches. A bit of forethought the previous night or morning allows for a quick and easy meal after a hard day's work on the farm. They're perfect for feeding a big group, so I tend to bring them out at harvest parties and butcherings, when crowds gather at the farm.

In a Crock-Pot, combine the roast, 1 teaspoon of the sea salt, the black pepper, and 2 teaspoons of the sweet paprika. Turn the heat to low and allow the roast to slowly simmer for about 8 hours, or until fork-tender.

While the roast is cooking, add the olive oil to a large pan over medium heat. When the oil is warm, add the onion and garlic. Gently cook for 5 minutes, until soft. Add the remaining sea salt, the red pepper flakes, the remaining sweet paprika, tomatoes, tomato paste, vinegar, molasses, cane sugar or maple syrup, and mustard. Stir to combine.

Cover and gently simmer the sauce for about 30 minutes. Taste it. *Really taste it.* Does it need more vinegar? More cane sugar? It's rare to find anyone who likes their barbeque sauce the same as the next person, so don't hesitate to adapt it a bit to your taste.

When the roast is fork-tender, carefully transfer it from the Crock-Pot to a plate and let it cool for a few minutes before you get in there and do your thing. Ain't nobody need no burnt fingers. When slightly cooled, use two forks to shred it. Remove any extra pieces of fat or bone (and save for stock!). Remove any extra liquid from the Crock-Pot (save this for stock, too!) and return the shredded beef back to the warm Crock-Pot.

Add the sauce to the Crock-Pot. Let the beef warm up for about 20 minutes before serving a healthy pile of the tender, juicy, shredded barbecue beef atop your bun of choice. I like to add some shredded cabbage or sauerkraut for texture.

CHICKEN PICCATA

Serves 4

Once upon a time, there was a girl who fell in love with a lemon chicken dish, and they lived happily ever after in culinary bliss. The end. What? You think I'm kidding? I'm totally not.

Pat the chicken dry with a clean dish towel. Sprinkle the flour over a shallow baking pan. Place the chicken pieces in the floured pan and gently move them around to coat completely in the flour.

Heat the olive oil in a large skillet. When the oil is shiny and hot, carefully place 4 of the flour-coated chicken pieces into the pan. Sprinkle with sea salt and black pepper.

Preheat the oven to 300°F.

Allow the chicken to cook for 5 minutes over medium-high heat, until crispy and golden. Turn over and cook the other side for 5 minutes, until a nice crust forms. Remove the first batch to an ungreased baking dish and repeat with the remaining chicken. When the second batch is cooked and nicely browned, transfer to the baking dish and place in the oven to continue cooking for 10 to 15 minutes, until the chicken is cooked thoroughly.

To the skillet that was used to brown the chicken, add the minced onion and garlic. Sauté for 3 to 4 minutes, or until just golden and soft.

Add the chicken stock. Follow with the lemon juice and lemon slices. Allow the sauce to simmer for 10 minutes, until slightly thick and sticky. Add the capers, butter, and parsley.

Remove the chicken from the oven. Just before serving (don't do it too soon or it will make the chicken crust soggy), pour the sauce over the chicken and sprinkle with more parsley, if desired.

8 boneless chicken thighs, or 4 chicken breasts, halved width-wise

¼ cup sprouted wheat flour or unbleached, organic all-purpose flour

4 tablespoons olive oil

Sea salt

Freshly ground black pepper

1 onion, minced

2 cloves garlic, minced

1 cup Chicken Stock (see page 64)

¼ cup freshly squeezed lemon juice

½ lemon, thinly sliced

3 tablespoons capers

3 tablespoons butter

Fresh parsley, for garnish

ONE-SKILLET BEEF AND POTATOES WITH GOAT CHEESE

Serves 4

1 pound ground beef

2 to 3 pounds fresh garden potatoes, cut into 1-inch pieces, skins on

3 cups greens, such as beet greens, collards, kale, or chard, roughly chopped

½ cup minced fresh parsley, thyme, and chives

Sea salt

Freshly ground black pepper

1 cup goat cheese, crumbled

1 tablespoon red wine vinegar, optional

This one-skillet lunch or dinner is anything but fancy. It's also not profound, difficult, time-consuming, or high-end cuisine. It's meat and potatoes for the farm laborers. Namely, myself and Stuart.

Brown the ground beef in a dry cast-iron skillet over medium-high heat. Add the potatoes, cover, and allow the potatoes to steam until fork-tender, about 15 minutes.

Toss in the greens and the herbs. Cover again and allow to steam for 5 minutes more. Transfer all to a large bowl. Season with salt and pepper. Sprinkle with the goat cheese and garnish with additional fresh herbs and a few splashes of red wine vinegar, if desired.

ROASTED CHICKEN IN MILK WITH CINNAMON AND LEMON

Serves 4–6

3 tablespoons butter

2 tablespoons olive oil

1 (3- to 5-pound) whole chicken

Sea salt

Freshly ground black pepper

Zest of 2 lemons, reserving a little zest for garnish

6 cloves garlic

1 cinnamon stick

5 cups whole milk

3 tablespoons parsley, minced, plus a little extra for garnish

Chicken slow-simmered in milk and spices. Sound funny? Well, it tastes totally delicious. Cinnamon and chicken is a flavor pairing that continually surprises and delights me. For even more fun, after the chicken has cooked, strain the sauce through a fine-mesh sieve and return it to the dutch oven. Add rice to the sauce, cover, and cook until tender. Serve alongside the chicken.

In a large dutch oven, melt the butter and olive oil together. When the butter–oil is very warm, place the chicken into the dutch oven and brown the entire bird, rotating it every 5 minutes or so to get a nice, evenly browned skin.

When the chicken is browned, turn it over so it's breast side down. Sprinkle generously with sea salt and freshly ground black pepper. Add the lemon zest, garlic cloves, cinnamon stick, milk, and parsley.

Preheat oven to 350°F. Cover the dutch oven with its lid and cook the chicken at 350°F for 60 minutes. Remove the lid and continue cooking the chicken for another 30 minutes.

Just before serving, garnish with additional parsley and lemon zest, if desired. And be sure to spoon some of that delicious milky broth over the top!

CREAMY CHICKEN PASTA WITH SHALLOT AND BASIL

Serves 4

I don't often serve pasta as a main dish, but when I do, it's usually this baby because it's creamy, bright, flavorful, and completely satisfying. My favorite pasta is made with einkorn flour, an heirloom variety of wheat that has remained unchanged for thousands of years.

Heat the butter in a large cast-iron skillet. Add the chicken and season generously with salt and pepper. Cook for 4 minutes per side, or until cooked through. Remove to a plate to cool. Into the hot skillet, add the shallot and bell peppers. Sauté for 5 minutes, until softened.

Cut the cooled chicken into roughly 4 strips per piece. Place the chicken strips back into the skillet with the shallot and peppers. Add the cream cheese and cream, stirring gently to combine.

Cover the skillet and simmer over low heat for 30 minutes.

During the last 10 minutes of simmering, boil the pasta in a pot of water until al dente. When the pasta is ready, drain it in a colander, and add to the skillet. Combine the chicken mixture and the pasta, stir in the diced tomatoes, and season with salt and pepper.

Garnish with fresh basil and a generous sprinkling of freshly grated Parmesan cheese.

2 tablespoons butter

4 boneless chicken thighs or 2 boneless breasts

Sea salt

Freshly ground black pepper

2 shallots, minced

2 red bell peppers, cut into strips

4 ounces cream cheese

1½ cups cream

1 pound einkorn fusilli pasta or pasta of choice

Filtered water

2 small tomatoes, diced

Fresh basil, for garnish

Freshly grated Parmesan cheese, for garnish

BEEF AND BELL PEPPER GOULASH

Serves 6– 8

2 tablespoons butter

1 (3- to 4-pound) chuck roast

Sea salt

Freshly ground black pepper

1 large red onion, cut into strips

1 tablespoon sweet paprika

1 tablespoon smoked paprika

1 teaspoon caraway seeds

4 large red, orange, or yellow bell peppers, cut into strips

2 cups chopped tomatoes

3 tablespoons raw apple cider vinegar

Filtered water

Oh my, how I love this simple and rustic one-pot dish. I only make it in season, when the peppers and tomatoes are sweet and ripe in the garden. Some things are best enjoyed as nature intended.

Preheat oven to 350°F.

Heat the butter in a large dutch oven. Add the roast, give it a generous pinch (or two, or three) of sea salt and pepper. Gently brown the meat on all sides. Remove to a plate.

Into the dutch oven, add the onion strips, sweet paprika, smoked paprika, and caraway seeds. Gently sauté the onion and spices for 10 minutes. Add the bell peppers and sauté for 2 to 3 minutes more.

Return the roast back to the dutch oven, nesting it down among the onion and peppers. Add the tomatoes and apple cider vinegar. Then add the filtered water halfway up the side of the roast.

Cover the dutch oven with its lid and continue cooking the roast at 350°F for 2½ hours, or until fork-tender. Serve with your favorite rice.

SCALLOPED HAM AND POTATOES

Serves 6–8

Because we cure our own hams from our own home-raised pigs, this isn't a dish that we enjoy as often as we'd like. Homemade ham takes time! But when we've got one cured and ready for consumption, this is the go-to recipe I bust out for the leftovers. It's the perfect dish to use up those scrappy bits that are much too delicious (and valuable!) to waste.

Preheat the oven to 350°F.

Using a mandolin or food processor, slice the potatoes into super-thin slices and set aside.

Melt 2 tablespoons of the butter in a large skillet. Add the onion and sauté for 10 minutes, until soft. Add the diced ham and allow it to mingle with the onion and warm up a bit.

In a small saucepan over medium heat, combine the cream, milk, and flour. Whisk to combine until completely incorporated and slightly thickened, about 5 minutes.

Use the remaining tablespoon of butter to generously grease a large baking dish. Layer in some of the potatoes, then some of the onion and ham mixture. Add another layer of potatoes and the remaining onion and ham. Add the final layer of potatoes. Pour the cream mixture over all. Cover with foil and bake in the oven for 45 minutes, or until the potatoes are fork tender.

Remove the foil and sprinkle on the cheese. Bake for 20 minutes more uncovered, until golden and bubbly. Season with salt and pepper and garnish with freshly minced parsley and thyme.

3 pounds assorted potatoes

3 tablespoons butter, divided

1 large onion, minced

4 cups ham, diced

1½ cups cream

1½ cups whole milk

¼ cup organic, unbleached, all-purpose flour

2 cups cheddar cheese, shredded

Sea salt

Freshly ground black pepper

Fresh parsley, for garnish

Fresh thyme, for garnish

SIZZLING STEAK WITH VINEGAR AND TOMATO DRESSING

Serves 4

Butter

3–4 grass-fed sirloin steaks, about 2 pounds total

Sea salt

Freshly ground black pepper

5 tablespoons olive oil

1 tablespoon raw cider vinegar

1 teaspoon dried oregano

½ teaspoon dried chile flakes

10–15 cherry tomatoes, fresh, canned, or preserved

Thick-cut sirloin steak, tomatoes from the garden, a few hits of fresh herbs, and a couple of pantry staples. Bliss. Sheer bliss.

Preheat a cast-iron skillet over medium heat and add just a teeny bit of butter, about 1 teaspoon.

Place the steaks on a clean tea towel to dry a bit. This will help them sear nicely in the pan. Season one side of each steak with salt and pepper. Place the seasoned side down in the hot skillet and cook for 3 to 4 minutes.

While the steaks are cooking, combine the olive oil, cider vinegar, dried oregano, chile flakes, a generous pinch of sea salt and black pepper, and the cherry tomatoes in a shallow baking dish.

Flip the steaks and cook for another 2 to 3 minutes, or until done to your liking (we like our steaks rare to medium-rare). They should have a nice sear from the skillet . . . mmm. That's what I'm talkin' about.

When the steaks are done, transfer them to the shallow baking dish and allow them to marinate in the olive oil dressing for 2 minutes per side. Remove the steaks from the dressing, transfer to a large cutting board, and cut into ½-inch slices. Place the steak strips onto a large platter, arrange the cherry tomatoes around them, and drizzle the meat with the remaining dressing. Served with roasted potatoes—classic!

BAY-ROASTED CHICKEN

Serves 4–6

There's something magical about this chicken. What comes out of the oven, all crispy and fragrant, seems more than just the sum of its parts. It's one of the first recipes in my repertoire that highlights bay leaves, a delicious aromatic not soon to be forgotten. For a stronger rub, omit the olive oil when you blend the spices in the spice grinder.

Preheat the oven to 350°F.

Blend the bay leaves, thyme, sea salt, peppercorns, and olive oil together in a high-powered blender until smooth. If needed, add a bit more olive oil so the herbs combine into a silky smooth liquid.

Place the chicken in a roasting pan. Insert the lemon halves into the body cavity. Pour the olive oil mixture over the chicken, using your fingertips to spread evenly. Roast in the oven for 2 hours, or until thoroughly cooked.

8 dried bay leaves

2 teaspoons dried thyme

1 teaspoon sea salt

1 teaspoon black whole peppercorns

⅓ cup extra-virgin olive oil

1 (3- to 5-pound) whole chicken

1 lemon, cut in half

KILLER PORK TACOS

Serves 6–8

1 (4- to 5-pound) pork roast, loin or shoulder

5 cloves garlic, minced

1 tablespoon sea salt

1 teaspoon ground cumin

1 teaspoon chili powder

1 teaspoon freshly ground black pepper

1 teaspoon dried oregano

½ teaspoon cayenne pepper

1 teaspoon cocoa powder

4 tablespoons raw apple cider vinegar

½ cup freshly squeezed orange juice

12 ounces beer of choice

Corn tortillas

Crumbled cheese, for serving

Tomato salsa, for serving

Sour cream, for serving

Sliced cabbage, for serving

If my husband could have his way, this might just be the only meal served on our farm. No matter how many times I serve it, it always satisfies him. I think it's because we get to eat it with our hands. Or maybe it's the beer-braised pork. Or perhaps the piles of toppings. Ah, who am I kidding? It's all good. Start the pork early in the morning, let it cook slowly all day while you work, and supper is a breeze.

Preheat the oven to 275°F.

Place the pork roast in a large roasting pan. Sprinkle with the minced garlic.

In a small bowl, combine the sea salt, cumin, chili powder, black pepper, oregano, cayenne pepper, and cocoa powder. Sprinkle the spice mixture over the roast, using your fingers to rub it into the meat.

Add the cider vinegar, orange juice, and beer to the roasting pan. Cover and bake in the oven for 6 to 7 hours, or until the pork shreds easily with a fork. Remove from the oven, let cool slightly, and shred the meat, removing any gristle or bone. Pour the liquid from the pan back over the shredded meat.

Serve a heaping scoop of the shredded pork atop a warm corn tortilla, topping it with crumbled cheese, salsa, sour cream, and sliced cabbage.

DIJON PORK CHOPS WITH GRAVY

Serves 4

4 large pork chops, about 1½ inches thick

¼ cup grainy Dijon mustard

¼ cup maple syrup

1 tablespoon raw apple cider vinegar

1 teaspoon sea salt

1 shallot, minced

3 cloves garlic, minced

½ teaspoon freshly ground black pepper, plus extra for seasoning the gravy

2 tablespoons lard or butter

2 tablespoons flour

1½ cups whole milk

Fresh parsley, for garnish

Our very first homegrown pork chops were served this way, and I've never looked back. The tang of the mustard and the sweetness of the syrup are the perfect combination for the pork's subtle flavor. I like to cut my chops into strips before serving so that they're easier to eat at the table . . . though the men in the family prefer to chew their meat off the bone. To each his or her own.

In a large, shallow dish, arrange the pork chops in a single layer.

In a small bowl, whisk together the mustard, maple syrup, vinegar, salt, shallot, garlic, and pepper. Pour the sauce over the pork chops and let them marinate in the refrigerator overnight, or for at least a few hours.

Preheat the oven to 200°F.

After marinating, heat a large cast-iron skillet over medium-high heat. Add the lard or butter and allow to melt. Remove the pork chops from the marinade and carefully place in the hot skillet. Cook for 3 to 6 minutes per side (use a longer cooking time for thicker chops) until golden and just barely pink inside. Transfer to a baking sheet and let rest in the oven for 10 minutes.

While the pork is resting, reduce the heat under the skillet to medium-low. Add the flour and whisk, scraping up any porky bits stuck to the bottom of the skillet. Add the milk and bring the gravy to a gentle simmer, whisking constantly, until thickened, about 3 minutes. Season with salt and pepper.

Remove the pork chops from the oven, transfer to a cutting board, and, using a sharp knife, cut the chops into ½-inch slices, maneuvering carefully around the bone. Place the strips on a plate, drizzle gravy over the top, and garnish with fresh parsley.

COD WITH SHALLOTS AND CREAM

Serves 4

6 tablespoons olive oil

4 shallots

2 or 3 pounds wild-caught cod

½ cup organic, all-purpose flour

Sea salt

4 tablespoons butter

4 tablespoons dry white wine

½ cup heavy cream

Freshly ground pepper, to taste

Parsley, for garnish

There's something about this dish that feels refined and fancy, even though it's made from basic ingredients. It feels impressive, the cod swimming in a shallot cream sauce and sprinkled gently with bright-green parsley. The perfect dish to impress a guest with.

Preheat oven to 200°F.

Heat the olive oil in a large cast-iron skillet over medium-high heat. Get it hot, baby. The trick to getting fish golden brown is to heat your oil and skillet properly before putting the fish in. You can tell it's ready for cooking when a dusting of flour into the oil sizzles rapidly and rises to the surface of the oil.

Slice your shallots thin and set them aside.

Lay the cod out on a piece of parchment (or the wrapper it came in). Sprinkle it liberally with the flour and a few generous pinches of salt.

Carefully place the floured cod into the hot oil . . . about 3 or 4 minutes per side is all. The cod should be nice and golden. Once it's cooked, move it to an ungreased baking sheet and place in a 200°F oven while you whisk together the sauce.

To make the sauce, reduce the heat before adding the butter. Then, add in the shallots. Let soften for about 5 minutes in the butter. After the shallots are soft, add in the wine. And then pour yourself a glass. Let the wine cook off for about 3 minutes in the pan at a low simmer while you drink a bit of yours.

Lastly, add in the cream and bring the entire mixture to a simmer before salting and peppering the sauce to taste.

To serve, place a piece of the fish on a plate, scoop a bit of sauce over it, and sprinkle with fresh parsley. This fish is delicious served alongside rice, pasta, grilled vegetables, or buttered potatoes

The Great Escape

"Your pigs are in my yard." This is one of the worst phrases any eight-months pregnant farmer could hear (especially knowing her husband was in town, enjoying some well-deserved chicken wings and beer with the guys). And yet here I stood at my door, at dusk, staring my neighbor in the face with a complete sense of disbelief. *My* pigs? *My* pigs had escaped?

Even though I'd just showered, applied my favorite relaxation oils, put a soothing station on the radio, and settled in with a mug of tea for the night, I quickly found myself bombing down our driveway . . . in my golfcart . . . and my pink bathrobe.

Perhaps the pigs knew what awaited them. After all, this was six months into our fattening them up for slaughter. With just eight weeks left to go before the dreaded day, perhaps they longed for one more adventure. One more chance at freedom. Unfortunately what they failed to realize is how long I'd been pining for bacon. And ham. And breakfast sausage. And though it is always bittersweet to butcher an animal you've raised for meat, most of us farmers simply don't have the financial means to let six months of feeding bills escape through the neighbor's yard. And so, the great chase began.

Thankfully the pigs were so large at this point they tended to waddle more than run and seemed to be quite content munching on

ground cover and bushes nearby. I say thankfully because at eight
months pregnant, I was also much too large to be running around
the hillside, hoping to spot a rogue hog. I'm sure it was quite a
sight—me with my rotund belly and pink bathrobe, waddling around
the mountainous terrain with two 275-pound pigs. Eventually I was
able to bribe them back to the barn with a bucket of Sal's milk and
grain where I remained, on the verge of tears and swearing, until my
husband arrived a short time later.

Don't worry. I got the last laugh. Mmm, mmm, mmm.

sweets

BLUEBERRY AND RHUBARB GALETTE

Serves 6

2 cups all-purpose einkorn flour (or sprouted whole-grain flours of choice), plus 1 tablespoon for fruit filling

3 tablespoons dehydrated whole cane sugar or sweetener of choice, plus ¼ cup for fruit filling

Generous pinch of sea salt

8 tablespoons cold butter, cut into small cubes

¼ cup ice water

1 cup rhubarb, cut into small pieces

1 cup fresh blueberries

1 egg white

1 tablespoon dehydrated whole cane sugar

I love galettes. They're far less fussy than pies, and less fussy is certainly more my style. This one is filled with blueberries and rhubarb, but you can fill yours with strawberries, peaches, spiced apples . . . any goodness your heart desires.

Preheat oven to 375°F.

Combine the flour, 3 tablespoons sugar, and sea salt together in a food processor. Pulse to combine and aerate. Add in the butter. Pulse to combine until the mixture reaches a sandy texture. Add the ice water, tablespoon by tablespoon, until the dough is just combined and sticks together when pinched. Gather all of the dough into a ball, wrap in parchment paper, and refrigerate for 30 minutes.

In another bowl, combine the rhubarb, blueberries, remaining sugar and flour together in a bowl. Stir to combine and coat the fruit in the sugar and flour mixture. Set aside.

Remove the dough from the refrigerator and heavily dust a work surface with flour. Use the palm of your hand to squish the dough into a rough circle shape before using a rolling pin to gently roll the dough ball into a 12-inch round, dusting with flour as necessary to keep the dough from sticking.

Place the dough on a sheet of parchment paper. Spoon the rhubarb and blueberry mixture into the center of the round, keeping a 3-inch border along the outside of the dough free of fruit. Begin to use your fingers to gently fold the edges of the dough inward toward the center of the circle, crimping and folding as necessary until all of the fruit is surrounded by folded crust.

Slide the parchment paper and the galette onto a baking sheet.

Whip the egg white in a small bowl with a fork before carefully brushing it onto the pastry edges of the galette with a pastry brush. Sprinkle the pastry edges with a few pinches of sugar, if desired.

Bake in the oven for 50 minutes or until set and golden. Allow the galette to cool before slicing and serving.

BLACKBERRY CUSTARD CAKE

Serves 6

I don't care how many dessert recipes call for cream and eggs, it will never be enough for me! These individual custard cakes are a wonderful and simple dish to make for guests—or little ones who squeal with delight at seeing the custard cakes rise and fall in the ramekins.

Preheat the oven to 350°F.

Butter six ramekins with your fingers, then dust lightly with flour.

Divide the berries evenly among the ramekins (unless you're selfish and prefer to fill up yours slightly higher. Not that any selfless, loving mother would do such a thing!).

In a blender or bowl, combine the cream, flour, sugar, maple syrup, eggs, and sea salt. Mix, mix, mix, mix for about 1 minute on low (in the blender) or 2 to 3 minutes (if whisking by hand).

Pour the custard mixture over the berries, dividing evenly among the ramekins.

Bake for 30 minutes, until the tops are just barely golden and the middle of the custards are still slightly jiggly. These are best served warm with a dusting of powdered sugar.

Butter, for preparing ramekins

2 cups fresh blackberries (or fruit of choice)

1 cup cream

½ cup organic, unbleached all-purpose flour, plus extra for preparing ramekins

¼ cup dehydrated whole cane sugar

1 tablespoon maple syrup

6 eggs

Pinch of finely ground sea salt

EINKORN BUTTER CAKE

Serves 6

3 cups all-purpose einkorn flour (or sprouted einkorn flour)

1 cup dehydrated whole cane sugar

16 tablespoons salted butter at room temperature (organic and pastured is best), plus extra for preparing the cake pan

7 egg yolks, divided

2 tablespoons rum, optional

Seeds from 1 vanilla bean, or 1 teaspoon vanilla extract

1 teaspoon cream

There's a fancy French name for this type of cake, Gâteau Breton, that I say when I'm trying to be sophisticated. But at the end of the day, it's butter cake. As in sixteen-tablespoons-of-butter butter cake. Yes, that's a lot of butter.

Preheat the oven to 350°F.

Butter and add parchment paper to an 8-inch round cake pan.

In a bowl, combine the flour and sugar. Whisk to combine. Add the butter, 6 egg yolks, rum if using, and vanilla seeds or vanilla extract. Use your hands to gently combine the mixture. Don't knead the dough, but rather lovingly and gently work your fingers through the ingredients until it's all incorporated together.

Transfer the dough to the cake pan and use your fingers to gently press the dough evenly into the pan, reaching all sides of the pan.

Combine the remaining egg yolk and the cream together in a small bowl before brushing it over the top of the cake. Score the top with a fork, if desired.

Bake for 30 to 35 minutes, until deeply golden. Let the cake rest for a few minutes before removing it to a wire rack to cool.

PÂTÉ SUCRÉE (SWEET DOUGH)

Makes enough for 1 (10-inch) tart shell

The base of many delicious desserts, pâte sucrée is a sweet dough that can be made quickly and utilized as needed. It freezes well and is a wonderful staple to have on hand. I use it as the base for chocolate ganache treats and even lemon tart. If you're desperate (cough) or pregnant, simply roll it out, sprinkle it with a bit of cinnamon and sugar, and bake until golden. I won't tell.

In a standing mixer, beat together the butter and cane sugar until creamy. Add the salt, egg yolk, and vanilla, mixing to combine. Add the flour, mixing just enough to combine the ingredients.

Wrap the dough in plastic wrap and refrigerator overnight, or for at least a few hours before using.

8 tablespoons butter, at room temperature

½ cup dehydrated whole cane sugar

¼ teaspoon sea salt

1 egg yolk

½ teaspoon vanilla extract

1¼ cups sprouted, all-purpose flour, or einkorn flour

CHOCOLATE CHIP BISCOTTI

Makes about 2 dozen biscotti

- ½ cup dehydrated whole cane sugar
- ½ cup honey
- 4 tablespoons butter, softened
- 2 eggs
- 1 teaspoon vanilla extract
- 2 cups all-purpose flour or einkorn flour
- 1 teaspoon baking powder
- ¼ teaspoon sea salt
- ¾ cup semisweet chocolate chips

There's nothing not to love about biscotti. They're crispy. They're sweet. They're salty. They're everything good served alongside a strong cup of espresso.

Preheat the oven to 350°F and line a baking sheet with parchment paper.

Combine the cane sugar, honey, and butter In a standing mixer and whip for 3 to 5 minutes on medium speed, until the mixture is light and fluffy. Add the eggs, one at a time, and continue mixing until just combined. Add the vanilla extract and whip to incorporate.

In a bowl, combine the flour, baking powder, and sea salt. Set the mixer on low speed and add the flour mixture a little bit at a time, until completely incorporated, scraping down the sides of the bowl as needed. Add the chocolate chips and mix by hand to incorporate.

Flour your hands, gently divide the dough in half, and place onto the parchment-lined baking sheet. Shape into two 3 × 10-inch logs. They'll be a bit sticky, which is fine. Just form the logs as best as you can. Long and skinny is the name of the game here.

Bake for 30 to 35 minutes, until golden. Remove from the oven and carefully transfer the biscotti logs to a wire rack for 10 minutes. Reduce the oven to 325°F.

After the biscotti are slightly cooled, transfer one of the logs to a cutting board. Using a serrated knife held at a 45-degree angle, slice the biscotti log into ½-inch pieces. Gently place the biscotti slices back onto the baking sheet and bake for 15 minutes more, turning them over halfway through the final baking process. Transfer back to the wire rack and let cool. Repeat with the second biscotti log. These cookies can be stored in an airtight container for up to a week.

CHOCOLATE GANACHE TARTLETS

Makes about 2 dozen tartlets

I shall never tire of eating these treats. Mama treats. For when Mama, y'know, needs a serious treat.

Preheat the oven to 325°F.

Break up the chocolate into small pieces and place in a large bowl. Heat the cream in a small saucepan until just boiling. Pour the cream over the chocolate pieces and let the mixture sit for 30 seconds. Gently mix together using a spatula, being careful not to whisk bubbles into the ganache.

While the cream and chocolate are mingling, roll out the pate sucree to a thickness of ¼-inch. Butter two 12-cup muffin tins. Cut circles of the Pâté Sucrée with a circle-shaped cookie cutter and line each muffin cup with a circle of the dough. Using your fingers, gently push the dough down into the bottom of each cup.

Place the tins in the oven and bake for 8 minutes to set the dough slightly. Remove from the oven, pour a bit of chocolate ganache into each tartlet, and return to the oven for another 8 minutes, until just set. The ganache should be slightly jiggly in the middle. Allow the tartlets to cool thoroughly before removing from the muffin tin.

4 ounces semisweet chocolate, preferably organic and naturally sweetened

⅔ cup heavy cream

1 recipe Pâté Sucrée (see page 169)

Butter, for preparing muffin tins

ESPRESSO-SPICED WALNUTS

Makes 5 cups (but they don't last long!)

For the walnuts:

5 cups walnuts, soaked and dehydrated

Filtered water

Sea salt

For the espresso spice mixture:

2 teaspoons ground decaf espresso

½ cup dehydrated whole cane sugar

3 teaspoons ground cinnamon

¼ teaspoon black pepper

½ teaspoon sea salt

2 egg whites

2 tablespoons vanilla extract

I delight in providing my family with finger foods like these walnuts, which are full of good fats and spiced enough to make them interesting. My little ones can't get enough of these walnuts. I love that I get to sneak handfuls before bed. The recipe takes a bit of time from start to finish, but don't let that deter you. It's very simple. Soaking the nuts wakes up the digestive enzymes within the nut and makes the nutrients more accessible and digestible. If you'd like to omit this step, simply start with shelled walnuts.

Place the nuts in a bowl and then pour in enough filtered water to cover them completely. Add a pinch of salt and let them soak for 12 hours.

Strain the nuts through a colander, spread in a single layer on a baking sheet, and then place in the oven on the lowest setting for about 12 hours, until the nuts are dry and crispy. Transfer to a large bowl.

Increase the oven to 300°F.

In a bowl, combine the espresso, sugar, cinnamon, black pepper, and sea salt. Mix to combine.

In a separate bowl, whisk the egg whites and vanilla until frothy. Pour the egg whites over the walnuts and gently stir to coat. Sprinkle the sugar mixture over the walnuts and stir to evenly coat all the nuts.

Spread the coated walnuts onto a parchment-lined baking sheet and bake in the oven for 30 to 40 minutes, stirring halfway through the baking time, until all are toasted and tasty.

CREAMY CARROT CAKE

Makes 1 standard loaf cake

This is my most favorite cake in the entire world. It's so moist and delicious. Plus, I love its rustic appearance. I've never been a fancy cake kinda gal anyway.

Preheat the oven to 350°F.

Combine the butter and sugar together in a standing mixer and whip until light and fluffy. Drizzle in the honey and continue to whip. Add the egg yolks one at a time, mixing continuously to incorporate. With the mixer still running, add the vanilla extract, all-purpose flour, sprouted flour, baking soda, cinnamon, nutmeg, allspice, cloves, pecans, and carrots. Continue mixing until thoroughly combined.

Pour batter into a generously buttered standard loaf pan and bake for about 50 minutes. Check for doneness by inserting a toothpick into the middle. If it comes out clean, it's done. If it's still gooey, bake for a few more minutes. Remove the cake from the oven and let rest for 10 minutes. Carefully move to a wire rack to cool. While it's cooling, prepare the icing.

To make the icing, whip together all the ingredients in a standing mixer until light and fluffy. Smear the cooled cake with the cream cheese icing and garnish with a bit of lemon zest and a few chopped pecans—because it looks pretty.

1 cup butter, at room temperature, plus extra for preparing loaf pan

¼ cup dehydrated whole cane sugar

½ cup honey

5 egg yolks

1 teaspoon vanilla extract

½ cup organic, unbleached all-purpose flour

½ cup sprouted flour

1 teaspoon baking soda

1 teaspoon ground cinnamon

⅛ teaspoon grated nutmeg

⅛ teaspoon ground allspice

⅛ teaspoon ground cloves

½ cup chopped pecans, plus more for garnish

1½ cups shredded carrot

Lemon zest, for garnish

For the cream cheese icing:

8 ounces cream cheese

¼ cup honey

1 teaspoon vanilla extract

INSTANT BERRY ICE CREAM

Serves 4

3 cups frozen berries

1 teaspoon vanilla

3 tablespoons, or to taste, maple syrup

½ cup heavy cream

Fresh berries, for garnish

Lemon zest, for garnish

My little ones still request this 100 times more than any other ice cream. It's such a wonderful way to enjoy a sweet treat without any of the artificial ingredients or flavorings of store-bought varieties. Bonus: You don't even need an ice-cream maker!

Combine all the ingredients together in a high-powered blender, pulsing to completely mix. This will be a thick mix for your blender, so stop it every 30 seconds or so to mix up the contents. It will be the consistency of a very thick smoothie. Garnish each serving with fresh berries and lemon zest.

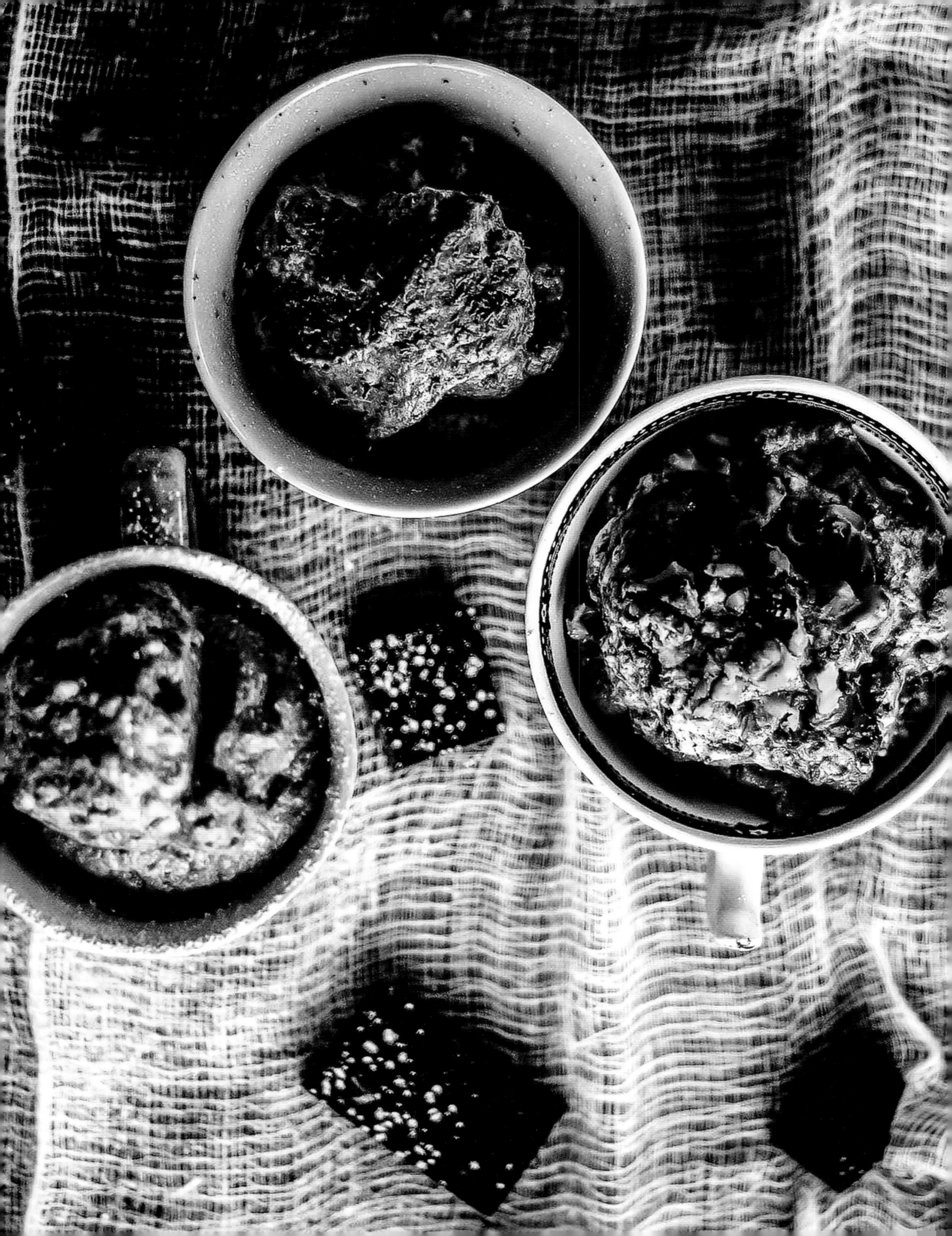

EASY CHOCOLATE MOUSSE

Serves 8

When I want a dessert that's sure to please, this is my go-to dish. It only takes a few minutes to whip up and is absolutely out of this world—especially when it's topped with bright red raspberries and chopped pistachios. Fuggedaboutit. We're using raw egg whites in this recipe, so source the best eggs you can get your hands on.

Combine the chocolate chips and butter in a heatproof glass bowl. Place the bowl over a saucepan filled with water and heat the saucepan over medium heat, to indirectly melt the chocolate chips and butter together.

Meanwhile, whip the cream in a standing mixer until fluffy and stiff. Transfer the whipped cream to a bowl and place the egg whites in the mixing bowl. Add a pinch of sea salt and whip the egg whites until stiff peaks form.

Add half the melted chocolate into the whipped cream and gently (and I mean *gently*!) fold to combine. The goal is to maintain maximum volume, so fold it together carefully. Then fold in the other half of the chocolate. Finally, fold in the whipped egg whites, and continue folding until entirely combined.

Refrigerate for 1 hour to set the mousse. Garnish with fresh fruit, chopped nuts, shaved chocolate, additional whipped cream, or whatever you little heart desires.

8 ounces semisweet chocolate chips

4 tablespoons butter

2 cups heavy cream, cold

3 eggs whites

Pinch of sea salt

Fresh berries, chopped nuts, shaved chocolate, or prepared whipped cream, for garnish

EARL GREY AND ROSE WATER COCONUT FLAKES

Makes about 2 cups

2 cups coconut flakes

⅓ cup honey

10 drops rose water

1 teaspoon Earl Grey
tea leaves

½ teaspoon orange zest

Teeny, tiny pinch of
sea salt

1–3 teaspoons water, hot

I love to keep a batch of these on hand for when I need a little sweet somethin'. Munch, munch, munch . . .

Preheat the oven to 275°F.

Place the coconut flakes in a large bowl.

In a small bowl, mix together the honey, rose water, tea leaves, orange zest, and salt. Whisk to combine. If the mixture is thicker than a syrup, add 1 teaspoon hot water and stir to thin it slightly. Pour the honey mixture over the coconut flakes and stir to combine.

Pour the sticky coconut flakes onto a parchment-lined baking sheet and bake in the oven for 20 to 25 minutes, until just barely golden. Remove from the oven and let cool. Nibble. Enjoy. Try not to be a glutton (points to self) and eat the entire batch in one sitting.

RED WINE AND HONEY-POACHED PEARS AND PLUMS

Serves 4

This is exactly the type of dessert I love—simple flavors, not in-your-face sweet, and full of complex richness without taking too much time to prepare. If you prefer to skip the oven method, simply add the fruit to the honey and red wine in a small saucepan and gently simmer over very low heat on the stovetop. Either way it's a mouthwatering winner.

½ cup honey

½ cup red wine

1 vanilla bean, sliced lengthwise

3 ripe pears

12 ripe plums

Preheat the oven to 350°F.

Combine the honey and red wine together in a small saucepan and bring to a gentle simmer, whisking to combine. Remove from the heat. Add the vanilla bean and stir. Allow the vanilla bean to mingle in the wine while you prepare the fruit.

Core the pears and slice 1-inch slices. Cut the plums in half and remove the pits.

Line a 9 × 11-inch pan with parchment paper, allowing for 4 inches of overhang on all sides. Place the fruit on top of the parchment paper. Gently pour the red wine mixture, including the vanilla bean, over the fruit. Carefully fold the parchment paper into a packet. I start by folding the top down and then fold the sides up. You can staple or tie them closed, if need be. Essentially what we're doing here is steaming the fruit in red wine. Yes, that's why this is so delicious.

Place the pan in the oven for 20 to 30 minutes until the fruit is fork-tender, allowing it to gently poach in the liquid. Serve with a generous scoop of vanilla ice cream, a big dollop of freshly whipped cream, or even by itself with an espresso. One simply cannot go wrong with such a dish.

LEMON TART

Makes 1 (10-inch) tart

1 recipe Pâté Sucrée
(see page 169)

4 eggs

4 egg yolks

1 cup honey

1 cup freshly squeezed
lemon juice

Zest from 3 lemons

¾ cup heavy cream

Powdered sugar,
for dusting

Lemon desserts are among my favorites. And this tart is among the very best of those! It's a constant request for birthdays around these parts, and I'm more than happy to oblige, because it means I get to enjoy a generously portioned slice . . . or four.

Preheat the oven to 350°F.

Roll the chilled pâté sucrée into a ¼-inch-thick disk. Carefully transfer to a 10-inch parchment-lined tart pan, using your fingertips to gently press the dough into the pan, while allowing the dough to overhang the pan's edges. Using a fork, poke a few holes into the bottom of the tart shell and chill in the freezer for 20 minutes. Bake for 20 to 25 minutes, until golden. Remove and set aside.

While the pâté sucrée is baking, whisk together the eggs, egg yolks, honey, lemon juice, and lemon zest until completely combined and smooth. (This is easiest to do in a standing mixer with the whisk attachment.) Allow the mixture to sit for 15 minutes before adding the cream and whisking again to gently combine. Strain the lemon mixture through a fine-mesh strainer to remove the zest.

Using your fingers, carefully break off the overhanging bits of tart shell so that the top of the shell is even with the top of the pan. Pour the lemon mixture into the prebaked tart shell and return it to the oven for 30 to 35 minutes, until the middle is set, but gently jiggly. Yes, that's what I said: gently jiggly.

Remove the tart from the oven and let cool completely before removing it from the pan. Slice, dust with powdered sugar, and demolish!

GOOSE EGG CUSTARD

Serves 4 to 6

Yes, we keep geese for their delicious, gigantic eggs. And yes, I've been known to mix those up into a decadent custard. There can never be too much cream in my life.

Preheat the oven to 325°F. Place a large baking pan in the oven and add enough hot water to fill to a depth of 1 inch.

Scald the milk by heating it in a saucepan until just barely simmering. Remove from the heat and allow it to cool slightly. Meanwhile, combine the eggs; rapadura, honey, or maple syrup; sea salt; and vanilla extract in a bowl, whisking to combine.

Slowly drizzle the scalded milk into the egg mixture. *Slowly. Slooowwwwllly!* (Trust me, if you add the milk too quickly, you'll end up with a bunch of scrambled goose eggs.) As you drizzle in the milk, stir constantly with a whisk, until all the milk is added. Pour the mixture into buttered ramekins. Place the ramekins into the water-filled baking sheet in the oven. Bake for 40 to 50 minutes, or until just set, slightly jiggly, and slightly browned on top.

Carefully remove the ramekins from the oven. You can serve this custard hot, warm, or cold. No matter how you eat it, it's delicious! I should know. I've eaten enough to be an expert.

4 cups whole milk, but no one will judge if you use cream, I promise

2 goose eggs

½ cup rapadura, honey, or maple syrup

Teeny pinch of sea salt

1 tablespoon vanilla extract

TAPIOCA PUDDING

Serves 6

⅔ cup tapioca pearls

1½ cups filtered water

4½ cups whole, organic milk

Large pinch of sea salt

3 egg yolks

½ cup raw honey

½ cup, or more, maple syrup

Beans from 1 vanilla pod, or 1 teaspoon vanilla extract

Tapioca pudding always makes me nostalgic. I remember my dad loving tapioca pudding and whenever I eat it, I think of him as a little boy, the youngest of five brothers, and how big of a treat it must have been to get a bowl of this squishy goodness. I can't ever get enough!

Combine the tapioca pearls and filtered water in a large saucepan. Set aside for 20 minutes to hydrate.

After the hydrating period the pearls will have soaked up the water. To them, add the milk, sea salt, and egg yolks. Bring the mixture to a low simmer and allow it to continue lightly boiling for about 10 minutes while stirring often.

Remove the pudding from the heat and whisk in the raw honey and maple syrup, adding more as desired. Let cool for about 15 minutes, and then fold in the vanilla beans or vanilla extract. Serve warm, at room temperature, or chilled. Oh, who am I kidding, it's delicious at any temperature!

When in Doubt

I remember the first time I tried to cook Stuart a cake, though frankly, I think I'd rather not. I hadn't much experience baking when we first got married, and though he was always kind enough to nibble my carrot muffins, they were certainly a far cry from the super-sweet baked goods he'd grown up with in Georgia. We couldn't have been more than six months into our married life before I began experimenting with a variety of flours, including sourdoughs, and soaked grains, trying to implement them into cakes I was already not very great at baking. So you can guess that the whole wheat sourdough birthday cake I made him wasn't exactly a keeper (the next year, he requested flan), but since that time, I've learned to master a less fussy take on cakes and treats (not to mention improved my skills significantly). Also, I've realized it's a lot harder to go wrong with sweet cream and eggs. When in doubt, flan it out.

a mix of
goodies

SMOKED HOLLANDAISE SAUCE

Makes about 2 cups

3 egg yolks

1 tablespoon freshly squeezed lemon juice

½ pound unsalted butter, melted and kept warm

Warm filtered water

Sea salt

Freshly ground black pepper

¾ teaspoon smoked paprika

½ teaspoon sweet paprika

I'll be honest here, I'm a total sucker for this hollandaise sauce. I'll drizzle it over practically anything, including eggs, grilled vegetables, crusty bread, chicken, you name it. Especially with that subtle hint of smoke from the paprika— yes, please!

Combine the egg yolks and lemon juice in a blender or food processor on low speed for 10 to 15 seconds. Increase the speed to medium and slowly drizzle in the warm butter, taking about a full minute to do so. Drizzling slowly is the key to a thick sauce. If the sauce becomes too thick, however, add a bit of the warm water (a teaspoon at a time) to achieve desired consistency.

Once the butter has been added, season the sauce to taste with salt and pepper.

Add the paprikas and blend for a few seconds to combine. Serve immediately.

PICKLED RED ONIONS

Makes about 2 pints

One of my most favorite condiments, these pickled red onions add a welcome zing to nearly any dish. Sometimes I put them on burgers. Sometimes I serve them alongside a roast chicken or even mix them into a green salad. Sometimes I eat them straight from the jar. There's no wrong or right way, my friends.

In a small saucepan, bring 3 cups water to a boil. Add the onion rings and blanch for 1 minute. Drain the water from the saucepan, leaving the onions.

Add the vinegar, sugar, pepper flakes, black pepper, and salt. Gently boil the onions in the vinegar mixture for 1 minute.

Transfer the onions and liquid to a jar, cover with a lid, and let cool to room temperature before refrigerating. The onions will keep in the refrigerator for 2 weeks.

Filtered water

2 medium red onions, peeled and sliced into rings

1 cup raw apple cider vinegar

3 tablespoons dehydrated whole cane sugar or honey

½ teaspoon red pepper flakes

½ teaspoon freshly ground black pepper

1 teaspoon sea salt

HOMEMADE BUTTER

Makes about 1 pound of butter, depending on the butterfat content of the cream

8 cups fresh cream (if using store-bought cream, try to find organic, grass-fed cream)

1 tablespoon buttermilk

Are you even kidding me? Could there be anything more delicious than fresh butter? The answer is no, at least as far as I'm concerned. Even if you're without your own dairy cow, source some cream from a local dairy and spend a few minutes making this. You won't be sorry.

Combine the cream and buttermilk in a bowl. Let sit at room temperature for 8 hours. This is the "culturing" part of cultured butter and is a fermentation process. During culturing, bacteria convert the milk sugars into lactic acid. The result is a much more flavorful butter.

After the culturing period, pour the cream into a stand mixer, food processor, or blender. On medium speed, allow the cream to whip. It'll start to look just like whipped cream, that's just what we're looking for! Keep going! Here's a breakdown of what you can expect: Cream. Whipped cream. Thick whipped cream. Lumpy whipped cream that will start to flick drops all over the counter. Weird, funky, chunky-looking whipped cream. Liquid with bigger chunks that no longer resembles whipped cream. Large chunks of butter floating in milky liquid.

When you get to that last stage, remove the butter chunks from the bowl and, using your hands, knead to combine, reserving the liquid. Run the butter under cold water and continue massaging and kneading the butter for 3 minutes, or until the buttermilk is no longer running out of the butter.

The buttermilk has a milk-like color, and it's important to get as much of it out of the butter as possible, as this will cause the butter to spoil quickly. Often I'll stick the entire slab of butter in a bowl of cold water and massage it gently. Then I'll dump the water out, refill the bowl with fresh water, and continue to massage until the water stays clear.

At this point, the butter can be eaten, salted, or frozen. I simply wrap my butterball up in a small piece of parchment and tuck it into the refrigerator. The reserved buttermilk should be refrigerated and used within a week.

FLAVORED BUTTERS

Makes ½ cup

The only thing better than fresh butter is punctuating it with various herbs, spices, and goodies. I love to keep flavored butter on hand for when a loaf of bread comes out of the oven and, well, I want to drown it in goodness. Grilled steaks are also the perfect canvas for herbed butters. Here are a few of my favorites. The preparation is the same for all of them.

Combine all the ingredients in a small bowl, smoosh together with the back of a spoon, roll into the shape of a log, and store in waxed paper or a covered container in the refrigerator until set.

Vanilla Bean and Berry Butter

- ½ cup freshly made butter, softened (see page 200)
- 2 tablespoons raw honey
- 2 tablespoons organic strawberry, raspberry, or berry preserves of choice
- Seeds of 1 vanilla bean

Lemon and Rosemary Butter

- ½ cup freshly made fresh butter, softened
- 1½ teaspoons lemon zest
- 1½ teaspoons minced fresh rosemary
- ½ teaspoon sea salt

Roasted Garlic and Sun-dried Tomato Butter

- ½ cup freshly made butter, softened
- 2 tablespoons feta cheese
- 1 tablespoon minced sun-dried tomatoes
- 1 clove roasted garlic, minced
- ½ teaspoon minced fresh chives
- Teeny pinch of sea salt

EASY HOMEMADE SOUR CREAM

Makes 4 cups

4 cups fresh cream

½ cup sour cream from previous batch (or organic, store-bought sour cream)

When one has access to raw cream from grass-fed cows as we do, it's a pure joy to make this homemade sour cream. All that it takes is culturing the fresh cream and a bit of time. The result is a cost-effective and probiotic rich sour cream that's perfect for topping a variety of dishes.

Pour the fresh cream into a glass jar. Add the sour cream culture into the fresh cream and stir to combine. Place a lid on the jar and allow the cream to culture at room temperature for 12 to 24 hours or to desired sourness. The sour cream can be refrigerated and eaten as-is or strained for a few hours through cheese cloth for an even thicker sour cream.

FLAVORED SALTS

Much like flavored butters, flavored salts are a very basic way to add some serious flavor to your simple dishes. I keep these three on hand at all times—in small, vintage dishes by the stove—for easy accessibility while cooking.

CUMIN SALT

Makes 3 tablespoons

2 tablespoons cumin seeds

1 tablespoon flaked sea salt

Gently toast the cumin seeds in a small saucepan over low heat for just a few minutes, until fragrant. Transfer to a mortar. Add the salt and, using the pestle, begin to grind the salt and cumin seeds together. Once they're fragrant and gently broken, transfer to a small dish for storage.

CHILI AND LEMON SALT

Makes 3 tablespoons

3 tablespoons sea salt

1 dried mild chile of choice, minced

Zest of 1 lemon

Combine the salt, chile, and lemon zest together in a mortar. Use the pestle to gently grind and combine the ingredients together. Transfer to a small dish for storage.

GARLIC SALT

Makes 1 cup

Preheat the oven to 250°F.

In a food processor, combine the garlic, salt, and parsley. Process until the ingredients are thoroughly combined and the consistency of sand.

Spread the salt on a parchment-lined baking sheet and bake in the preheated oven for 50 to 60 minutes, or until dry to the touch. Remove from the oven and let cool to room temperature. If needed, the garlic salt can be returned to the food processor after baking. A few quick pulses will easily break it up and achieve that sandy texture again.

Store in an airtight container.

7 fresh cloves garlic, peeled

1 cup sea salt

¼ cup fresh parsley

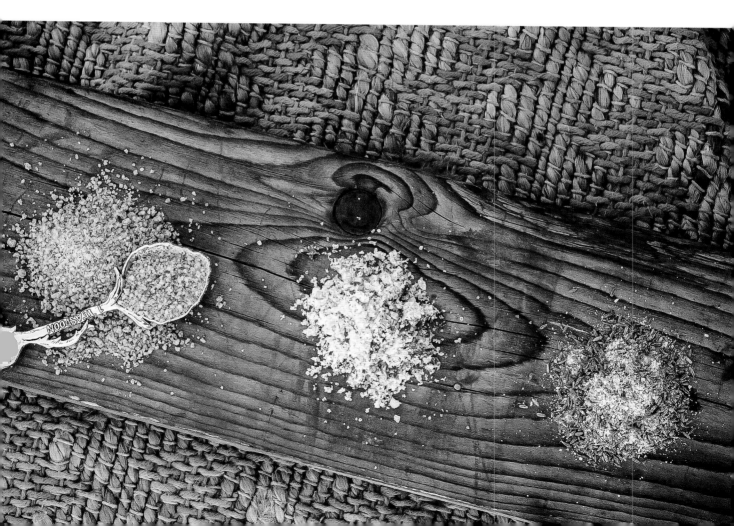

TUSCAN DIPPING OIL

Makes 1½ cups

I'll never get tired of dipping freshly baked bread into herbed oil. Never! For the best dipping oil, use the highest-quality olive oil and balsamic vinegar you can find. In the winter you can easily substitute dried herbs for the fresh ones; just cut the amounts by half, or to taste, because dried herbs can be a bit more potent than fresh.

In a small serving bowl, use a fork to combine the red pepper flakes, basil, rosemary, garlic, oregano, salt, and pepper. Drizzle in the olive oil. Lastly, drizzle in the balsamic vinegar. Gently whisk with the fork to combine. Allow the oil to sit for a few hours for the best flavor. Dip in your favorite crusty bread and enjoy!

½ teaspoon red pepper flakes

1 teaspoon minced fresh basil

1 teaspoon minced fresh rosemary

1 teaspoon minced garlic

1 teaspoon minced fresh oregano

¾ teaspoon sea salt

1 teaspoon freshly ground pepper

1 cup high-quality olive oil (For the love of all things, make it the best you can find!)

½ cup high-quality balsamic vinegar

GREMOLATA

Serves approximately 4

4 tablespoons fresh parsley

1½ teaspoons lemon zest

2 garlic cloves

There are millions of ways to make gremolata, which is Italian for a chopped herb condiment, but this one happens to be my favorite. It brings dishes to life and looks pretty while doin' it. If you're without a food processor, just do some chopping by hand. It will store for a few days in the refrigerator fairly well, but is best served fresh.

Combine the ingredients in a food processor and pulse to combine. Serve atop vegetables, meats, or potatoes.

DILLED CARROTS

Serves approximately 12

Another wonderful probiotic-rich condiment, these dilled carrots can be served alongside a meal just like kraut or pickles. They take just a few minutes to put together, and in a few days' time yield billions and billions of beneficial bacteria for your gut! I like to keep a jar in the refrigerator at all times.

Peel the garlic and gently smoosh the cloves. Transfer to a clean glass jar (a quart-size mason jar is perfect). Add the dill and sea salt.

Peel the carrots and then cut them into smaller pieces. Fill the jar with the carrot slices, making sure no carrots stick out of the top.

Top the jar off with filtered water, leaving 1 inch of headspace at the top of the jar.

Cover the jar with a lid and allow the carrots to ferment at room temperature for 3 to 4 days before transferring to the refrigerator. The carrots will keep for up to a year.

2 cloves garlic

1 tablespoon fresh dill, chopped

1½ tablespoons sea salt

6–10 carrots, depending on size

Filtered water

BARREL PICKLES

Each gallon contains 75 servings

Pickling cucumbers, about 75 for each gallon-size jar

Fresh dill

Garlic cloves

Onion

Peppercorns

Grape leaves (these keep the pickles crisp), from your backyard grapevines or the grocery store

Filtered water

Sea salt

In the old days, pickles were traditionally preserved in large barrels that would remain in a home's root cellar for the duration of the winter. I imagine a woman trudging down to the cellar with a bowl in hand to scoop out the daily pickle ration. These pickles are fermented and thus do an amazing job of supporting the beneficial bacteria in our guts. This is ideal for the long winter, when our immune systems are at their weakest.

Pick through the cucumbers and remove any that are moldy, squishy, or damaged. Only the best should make it into the crock. You can gently rinse them in water, if you need to remove dirt or debris.

Fill a gallon-size crock or glass jar half full of cucumbers before laying in a few sprigs of fresh dill, a clove of garlic, a chunk of onion, a pinch of peppercorns, and a few grape leaves. Stop it. I can hear you complaining. Yes, I realize this is vague, but that's okay. They're your pickles, and you can spice them however you like! I haven't noticed a big difference between using precise measurements or being random about it.

Fill a quart jar with filtered water and 1½ tablespoons sea salt. Stir to dissolve the salt and pour this over the cucumbers. Continue to fill the quart jar with this same proportion of water and salt until the crock is full and the cucumbers are completely submerged in the liquid.

Place a crock weight (or plate if you don't have one) over the top of the pickles so that they remain completely submerged during the course of their fermentation. You can also layer on some grape leaves to help protect the cucumbers from oxygen.

Allow the pickles to ferment on your countertop for 3 to 5 days, checking each day for mold on the surface of the brine. As long as the cucumbers remain submerged in the brine, they will be fine, have no fear! Once they are seasoned and fermented to your taste, move the crock to cold storage (or your refrigerator). The pickles will keep through the winter if kept cold.

CILANTRO AIOLI

Serves approximately 6

I call it cilantro, but really, this basic aioli can be made with any fresh herb you've got on hand, like thyme, basil, or dill. Use it in any way that you would mayonnaise—as a vegetable dip or as a topping for sandwiches or burgers. The aioli can be mixed by hand, but make sure you've got a big ol' whisk and some serious biceps. It will store well in the refrigerator for a few days in a covered container. Because we're using raw eggs in the recipe, it's essential you find the freshest ones available from a local farmer.

In a high-powered blender, combine the egg yolks, lemon juice, garlic, mustard, and cilantro. On medium speed, blend until the ingredients are combined.

Crank the blender up to high speed to emulsify the ingredients. While they're blending, slowly begin to drizzle in the olive oil. The mixture will begin to thicken and become very smooth. Continue to add the olive oil until the desired texture is achieved.

If you don't have a high-powered blender, make a garlic paste by smooshing the garlic and a pinch of salt with the side of a large knife and finely chop the cilantro. Combine the garlic paste, egg yolks, lemon juice, mustard, and chopped cilantro together in a bowl and whisk by hand. Add a small bit of olive oil at a time, continuing to whisk aggressively until the desired texture is achieved. This is how the old-timers used to do it!

4 egg yolks

2 tablespoons freshly squeezed lemon juice

½ clove garlic

1 tablespoon Dijon mustard

3 tablespoons fresh cilantro

1¼ cup extra-virgin olive oil

BASIL PESTO

Makes about 2 cups

2 cloves garlic

4 cups tightly packed
fresh basil leaves
(no stem or flowers,
please!)

¼ cup cubed Parmesan
cheese

1 cup olive oil

½ cup almonds, pine
nuts, or walnuts

Sea salt to taste

Pesto is a simple flavor booster and easy condiment to whip up fresh at home. If you're growing basil in your summer garden, it's the perfect way to use it all up. Served over grilled vegetables, meats, pasta, or boiled potatoes, it's simply magic.

In a small skillet over medium heat, gently toast the garlic cloves (with their skins still on) until just golden and fragrant. Let cool a bit and then peel the skin from the cloves.

In a high-powered blender or food processor, combine the garlic cloves, basil, Parmesan, olive oil, and nuts. Blend on high speed until very smooth, scraping down the sides of the blender or food processor if necessary. Personally, I really don't love chunky pesto, so I make sure to really blend it well. Blend, baby, blend.

Taste the pesto and season with a small pinch of sea salt, if necessary. Spoon the fresh pesto into jars and refrigerate or freeze.

RHUBARB CHUTNEY

Makes 6 pints

Most people don't know what to do with rhubarb. I get it. It's a weird pink stalk. Is it a fruit? Or a vegetable? Who's really sure? What I am sure of is that this rhubarb chutney is the perfect accompaniment for pork and chicken. It's easy enough to throw together in a large stockpot when rhubarb is in season and will keep in your refrigerator all through the winter months. It's salty, sweet, and sour . . . perfect to pair with fatty meats.

Combine all of the ingredients in a large pot. Slowly bring to a simmer. Allow the chutney to gently simmer for 30 minutes, until it cooks down and becomes thick. Stu's a more chunky-chutney person, so he likes his cooked down less. I'm a less chunky-chutney person, so I like mine cooked down a bit more.

Once the chutney is ready, ladle it into glass jars.

Once cooled, transfer the chutney to the refrigerator. This makes a pretty big batch, so freezing some may also be a good option if refrigerator space is limited. If kept in the refrigerator, it is best used up within 6 months.

2 pounds rhubarb stalks, cut into ½-inch pieces

2 cups honey

1 cup raw apple cider vinegar

1 cup dried cherries

1 teaspoon cinnamon

1 teaspoon sea salt

½ cup onion, finely chopped

2 teaspoons finely grated fresh ginger

1 dried chile pepper, minced, or ½ to 1 teaspoon red pepper flakes

SOURDOUGH STARTER

Makes 1½ cups

1 cup organic, unbleached all-purpose flour

¾ cup warm water

A healthy sourdough starter is the beginning of many delicious sourdough baked goods, from breads, to waffles, to crackers. Keeping one on hand takes little effort and provides your family with naturally leavened baked goods, full of beneficial bacteria and wild yeasts. Keep your starter on your counter, perhaps in a crock with a lid, where you'll remember to tend to it each morning.

Combine the flour and water in a small bowl. Mix with a spoon continually until well combined. The dough should be somewhat liquidy but not watery.

Place the dough in a large container, such as a gallon glass jar, and cover with a lid so it doesn't dry out. Allow it to sit for 12 hours. After 12 hours, feed your starter again with the same measurements of flour and water. Stir to combine, place back into the container, and allow it to sit again at room temperature.

Continue to feed your starter in this manner for 5 days. At this time it should be bubbly and smell slightly sour. That's a good thing!

To maintain your starter each day, combine 1 cup flour with ¾ cup warm water and ¼ cup of the healthy, bubbly sourdough starter. The remaining starter can be fed to your chickens or used to make Sourdough Skillet Bread (see page 47) and other delicious recipes.

AFTERWORD

*A*t the end of a meal, when the last bit of crumbs have been swept off the table and the wine glasses have been washed and stacked in the cabinet, we like to "light the candle" in the kitchen. The funny part is that we don't actually light a candle, but rather, we clean the counters, put fresh flowers in the old Le Parfait jar that sits on Madame (yes, I named my French cooking range), open the windows to let in the fresh air, and straighten the flour canisters so that they line up just so. To us, lighting the candle means we're preparing the kitchen, yet again, for the next meal. The next gathering. The next feast. While we wait, we take off our aprons, make an espresso, and pretend like life is just as orderly and fresh as the newly cleaned kitchen.

It never lasts longer than thirty minutes. Around these parts, it's almost *always* time to eat.

ACKNOWLEDGMENTS

*T*his book has been with me for years—both on my plate and in my heart. There are countless people behind the scenes helping make all of the pieces come together in the most beautiful way possible, and for that I'm filled to the brim with gratitude.

To Stuart, my much better half, for eating, washing dishes, and continually encouraging me to chase my wildest dreams. You are selfless, wise, and full of life. I love you beyond measure.

To my littles—Georgia, Owen, Will, and Juliette—for giving me the very best reasons to cook, to serve, and to laugh in the face of disaster. You'll never know how much we love you all.

To my entire extended family, for sharing so many meals with me and giving me many reasons to smile. This all takes a village and y'all are mine.

To Holly, my steadfast editor, for spending countless hours poring over these words, challenging me to be a better version of myself, and teaching me how to properly use the English language. Bless you for your patience, my friend.

To the entire Lyons Press team who has worked to make this book a beautiful reality, for believing in this project.

To Sally and the team at the Lisa Ekus Group, for making the magic happen.

And to my King, who has given me a heart for food and fellowship.

INDEX